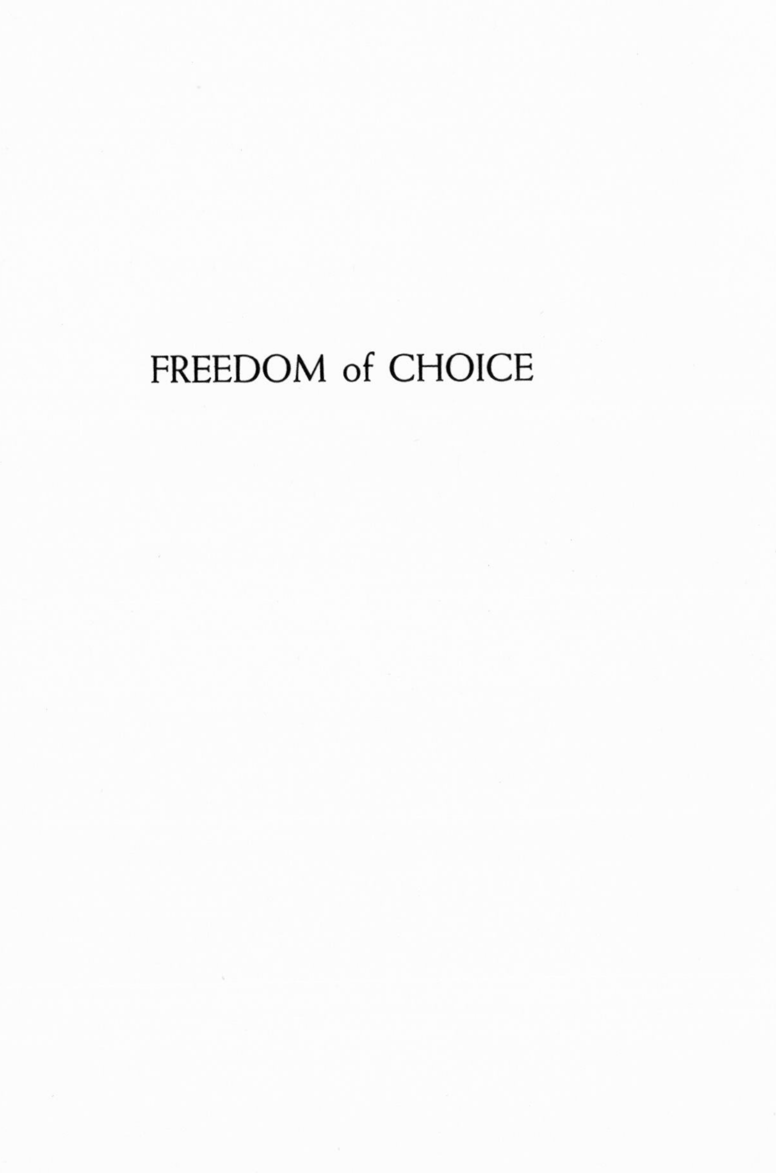

FREEDOM of CHOICE

BY THE SAME AUTHOR

The Tradition of Natural Law
edited by Vukan Kuic
FORDHAM UNIVERSITY PRESS, 1965

Freedom and Community
edited by Charles P. O'Donnell
FORDHAM UNIVERSITY PRESS, 1968

A Bibliography will be found on page 159.

FREEDOM of CHOICE

by Yves R. Simon

Edited by
Peter Wolff

with the assistance of
PAULE SIMON · DESMOND FITZGERALD

Foreword by
Mortimer J. Adler

New York
Fordham University Press
1969

Library of Congress Catalog Card Number: 75–75040
SBN 8232–0840–0

PRINTED IN THE UNITED STATES OF AMERICA

Contents

Foreword

Of all the questions or issues concerning human freedom, none is more fundamental in itself and in its consequences than the problem of free choice; and none has been the subject of more persistent and, at the same time, apparently irresolvable controversy. The parties to the controversy—the determinists, on the one hand, and the exponents of free will, on the other—have engaged, for the most part, in denials of positions that they attribute to their opponents but that their opponents do not hold.

While such blindness or failure of understanding can be found on both sides of the dispute, it must be said that the determinists are more egregious in their misunderstanding of the freedom the existence of which they deny—almost to the point of caricaturing it by identifying it with chance, claiming that it violates the principle of causality or sufficient reason, or asserting that it is a vacuous indeterminancy. It must be added that the fault is not wholly theirs, for their misunderstanding is in large part owing to the excesses and defects of the philosophers who have tried to explain why they attribute freedom of choice to man but who have failed to make that freedom intelligible or reasonable, and so have encouraged, if not actually justified, the caricature.

Here, with regard to this, as in other philosophical matters, it is useful to divide the history of Western thought by a line that separates the predecessors of Hume and Kant from their successors. Before Hume and Kant, the first and only satisfactory explanation of man's freedom of choice is that developed in the writings of Thomas Aquinas. When such freedom is denied by Hobbes, Spinoza, and Leibniz, or later by Priestley and Hume, the arguments that they advance take no account whatsoever of the grounds or reasons that Aquinas offers for affirming it. The amazing but incontrovertible fact is that these later philosophers proceed in total ignorance of his explanation of man's freedom of choice. And when, in the disputes of the seventeenth and eighteenth centuries, free will is defended against the determinists by Descartes, Bishop Bramhall, Locke, and Kant, the arguments that they advance either go too far or do not go far enough. In either case, they fail to give an account of free choice that has the intelligibility or reasonableness to be found in the doctrine of Aquinas. They, like their opponents, evince no awareness of that doctrine's existence.

In the centuries since Hume and Kant, the dispute between the determinists and the free-willists has proceeded along the same lines. Ingenuity has added new twists here and there, but in the main the followers of Kant have made free will less rather than more intelligible, and the followers of Hume have either repeated or exaggerated his caricature of free will. The current debate on the subject is no different—with one outstanding exception. That one exception is the present work. It is the only major essay on free choice written in this century that illuminates the controversy. It explains man's freedom of choice in a way that makes it compatible with all the findings and conclusions of modern science, and shows how the modern determinists are justified in rejecting the only versions of it with which they were acquainted, while at the same time it persuasively solicits their effort to understand a doctrine that they could not so easily reject—not, at least, if they were ever able to understand it.

Of the writers who continue to fill the philosophical journals with denials of free will, none, to my knowledge, is acquainted with Yves Simon's *Traité du libre arbitre*. They are still attacking the preposterous versions of free will that Hobbes and Hume attacked. Since the writings of Aquinas on the subject are and probably always will remain a closed book to them, this treatise by Yves Simon, a revision and translation of the French work, provides the only remedy that could possibly be effective in lifting the controversy to a more fruitful plane, for it not only expounds the doctrine of Aquinas in terms that are accessible to contemporary thinking, but it also employs an imagery that is consonant with contemporary discussion and elaborates the Thomistic doctrine in the light of contemporary psychology, including the insights of Freud.

Until now, Yves Simon's treatise of free choice has not been available in English. Mr. Wolff, who edited Yves Simon's translation, explains in his Preface the occasion that prompted his doing it—the research on freedom in which he took part as a member of the staff of the Institute for Philosophical Research in San Francisco. That research was the basis of my writing the two-volume study,

The Idea of Freedom, published in 1958 and 1961. The second volume contains a three-hundred-page exposition of the controversy concerning man's freedom of self-determination—his freedom of choice. Because the self-imposed discipline of the Institute requires its approach to philosophical controversy to be dialectically non-partisan or neutral, presenting all points of view without embracing or endorsing any, I could not in writing that portion of *The Idea of Freedom* say of Yves Simon's contribution what Mr. Wolff says about it in his Preface or what I have said in this Foreword. Writing this Foreword has afforded me the pleasant opportunity to cast aside those dialectical restraints and to express my own philosophical commitment to the conception and explanation of free choice that Yves Simon so brilliantly and persuasively expounds in this little book. Having performed the dialectical task of reviewing the whole literature of this subject—certainly, all the major arguments for and against free will—I feel secure in my estimate of the importance of Yves Simon's contribution.

This book, as I have said, is the perfect antidote for the errors, the misunderstandings—or worse, the ignorances—that beset the modern discussion of free choice. Even a reader who comes to this book with little or no knowledge of the philosophical literature on the subjects that it treats cannot fail to appreciate its remarkable clarity, its felicitous combination of detailed concreteness with abstract precision, its exploration of common experience and its elucidation of common sense, and, above all, the intelligibility, reasonableness, and fairness of its exposition of free choice not only in the context of opposing views but also in the context of all relevant psychological, ethical, and metaphysical considerations—the meaning of voluntariness and of responsibility, the role of the passions, the promptings of desire and the aspirations of love, the pursuit of happiness, the limitations of reason, the aspirations of the will, and the several principles of causality in their relation to one another and as they operate in the realms of matter and spirit or in the singularly human conjunction of body and mind.

MORTIMER J. ADLER

Aspen, Colorado
July, 1968

Editor's Preface

THE PROBLEM OF FREE CHOICE—or of freedom of the will as it has traditionally been called—is one of those persistent themes of philosophic inquiry that will not be put to rest. No matter how often the problem has been asserted simply not to exist, no matter how contemptuously it has been referred to again and again as a pseudo-problem, no matter how condescendingly the problem is said to have been solved long ago—the problem persists and exerts a continuing fascination on both the professional philosopher and the inquiring layman.

But if there is no lack of books that continue to deal with the problem and no paucity of those who consider its solution of profound importance, there is nevertheless a surprising and disappointing shortage of works that meet the problem of free choice squarely and lucidly. I became aware of this state of things while serving as Assistant Director of the Institute for Philosophical Research in San Francisco, when that organization was completing its research on the problem of "Freedom" which was later to result in the two-volume work *The Idea of Freedom* (Garden City, New York: Doubleday, 1958 & 1961).

In researching the philosophical literature on freedom of choice, I was struck by how few were the works that really carried out their promise of attempting to come to grips with, let alone solve, the "problem" of free choice, whatever it might be. But among the works of contemporary philosophers, there was one which stood out from all the rest, because it *did* identify what the author conceived to be the problem, because the author did indicate within what philosophical framework he hoped to find the answer to the question he had posed, and because he then set about demonstrating his solution. That work was *Traité du libre arbitre* by Yves R. Simon, published at Liège in 1951.[1] In writing the chapters of *The Idea of Freedom* dealing with free choice,

[1] Imprimerie Georges Thone, Liège, Belgium.

we relied greatly on Professor Simon's exposition. Because *Traité du libre arbitre* had not been translated into English, I prepared, for my own use, a translation of several of its crucial chapters, so that we might quote from the book with ease.

With so much of the work of translation already done, it occurred to me to write to Professor Simon and ask whether he had ever thought of having his book translated into English and whether he would like me to proceed with such a task. In replying, Professor Simon revealed that he was then engaged in an ambitious task, that of writing a multi-volume "Philosophical Encyclopedia" which would deal with most of the important philosophical problems. Free choice was to be one of the problems treated, in volume eight of the projected encyclopedia, and he himself was even then engaged in revising and translating *Traité du libre arbitre* in order to extract from it what he wanted for the new work.

Even at the time of writing to me, Professor Simon knew himself to be incurably ill and he asked me if, should it happen that he himself were unable to complete the task, I might undertake finishing the job. After Professor Simon's death, Mrs. Simon again urged me to edit the incomplete manuscript. Because of my high opinion of Professor Simon's work, I accepted.

Here, then, is the finished work. Professor Simon himself was able to revise approximately the first half of the book (Chapters 1 and 2). The last chapter, containing the most crucial sections of the book, had received only a cursory revision by him; it is an almost literal translation of the corresponding chapters from *Traité du libre arbitre*. From another part of the projected encyclopedia (Vol. 16, "The Matter and Form of Morality"), I have added a brief section, beginning on p. 152, to serve as a summary and conclusion.

In editing, I have been conscious of my duty of making as few changes as possible, since Professor Simon himself was not here to approve or disapprove them. For the most part, I have merely tried to decide which of several versions of the manuscript was the latest; I have added footnote references where possible. I have also occasionally changed sentences around a little, where they seemed to me to be a little too Gallic in structure and tone. At the same time I must confess to being rather fond of some of Professor Simon's Gallicisms and of having left some of them in the final version.

Great thanks are due to my co-editors, Professor Desmond FitzGerald of the University of San Francisco and Mrs. Paule Simon. Both have helped with the footnotes and have given me valuable help as to style and content. Final responsibility for any errors must of course remain mine. I should also like gratefully to acknowledge the help of my secretary, Mrs. Patricia Marasco, who typed the final manuscript and aided me in innumerable details.

PETER WOLFF

Sudbury, Massachusetts
March, 1968

FREEDOM of CHOICE

1

Introduction

IMAGES OF DISORDER

THE NOTION OF FREEDOM is commonly accompanied by powerful images: these should be identified at the very outset of our inquiry, lest they exert an uncontrolled influence on the shaping of our concepts and the statement of our problems. The popular imagery of freedom in uninhibited expression—that is what we need.

We can expect to find this expression in early Romanticism. Upon his arrival in Philadelphia a young disciple of Rousseau was astonished not to find in his hosts "the rigidity of the first Roman manners" [1] which, from the shores of the old world, he had attributed to them. But in the wilderness he could not fail to find the thing he was looking for: "Primitive Liberty! At last I recover thee. I move like the bird that flies before me: his directions are random, and nothing bothers him save the choice of his shelters. . . ." [2]

Many boast of loving liberty, yet almost no one has a proper understanding of it. When, in my travels among the Indian nations of Canada, I left the European settlements and found myself, for the first time, alone in the middle of a sea of forest, a strange revolution took place in my soul. In the kind of delirium which got hold of me, I was not following any track; I was going from tree to tree, to the right and to the left indifferently, and I was saying to myself: here, there are no more ways to be followed, no more cities, no more narrow homes, no more presidents, republics or kings, above all, no more laws, and no more men. Men here? Yes, a few good savages who do not bother about me anymore than I do about them; who—again like me—wander freely where thought drives them, eat when they want to, and sleep where and when they

[1] René de Chateaubriand, *Voyage en Amérique, Oeuvres complètes* (Paris: Panthéon littéraire, 1837) Vol. II, p. 21.
[2] *Ibid.*, p. 34.

please. And to test whether I was at last reinstated in my original rights, I elicited a thousand acts of will which infuriated the tall Dutchman who served as my guide and who, in his soul, believed that I was crazy.[3]

Who would disagree with the Dutch guide? And yet few have a right to contend that they always rejected as ungenuine the concept described here with all the candor of youthful romanticism. The dialectic of the whole issue is often biased from the beginning by the postulate of a conflict between order and freedom. For those fascinated by order, the treatment of freedom consists, at most, of reluctant concessions. But the lover of freedom claims that any excess in the administration of order destroys both freedom and life. Thus, on either side, freedom is interpreted as something disorderly, exuberant, lavish, inventive, creative, and insane, which gives all things color and warmth but carries a threat of universal chaos.

The proposition that disorder, or a tendency to bring about disorder, pertains to the essence of freedom is often expressed or understood in the treatment of moral, political, and pedagogical issues;

[3] *Essai historique sur les Révolutions*, Part II, ch. 57 in *loc. cit.*, Vol. I, p. 206. It is fair to report that in a later edition Chateaubriand acknowledged the foolishness of these early writings and confessed that good savages sometimes fed on the flesh of other good savages.

it also appears very often in the less impassioned discussions of the physicists and philosophers of nature. Most scientists hold that freedom, if tolerated anywhere, would jeopardize the orderliness of the scientific universe. Aversion to disorder is the real motive of their faith in unqualified determinism. Indeed, according to the dictates of our imagination, *a free act is an event without cause, an exception to the law of causality* and to the principle of uniformity in natural occurrences (*principe de legalité, Grundsatz der Gesetzlichkeit*). Such a thing cannot exist. Thus, at the end of a long inquiry, Sir James Jeans declares that freedom is but the unconscious determination of a man's action by his character and his personal history. He acknowledges a freedom from coercion, a freedom from determination by external forces, which is by no means incompatible with necessity, a freedom which consists in a necessary determination from within. As an alternative to this conception, the only thing that Sir James Jeans can think of is a whimsical way of acting, whose notion contradicts the data of consciousness as well as the requirements of reason.

If something determines his choice, we are back to determinism; if nothing, he acts from pure caprice, and this leads to a free-will which is neither of the kind we want to find nor of the kind we feel we do find. We like to imagine that we hold determinism at bay by our wisdom or virtue or foresight, and not through a mere random caprice over which we have no control and so for which we are in no way responsible. . . .

Neither does a capricious indeterminism give us a free-will at all resembling that of our experience or imagined experience. If every event were not determined by a sufficient reason, the whole world would, as Leibniz remarked, be a chaos. A mind endowed with a free-will of the capricious variety would be a prey to spontaneous and wholly irrational impulses; we should describe it as the mind of a madman, although in actual fact no madman's mind is ever quite so crazy. The further psychology and common sense probe into the question, the more necessary they find it to accept orthodox determinism—our acts are determined by our volitions, our volitions by our motives, and our motives by our past.[4]

The Epicurean theory constitutes a daring pattern for all philosophies that identify freedom with causal indetermination, or at least place the beginning of freedom in the indetermination of natural events. Epicurus is a moralist who needs a certain vison of physical nature in order to carry out a moral reformation aimed at peace of mind and heart. To under-

[4] *Physics and Philosophy* (New York: Macmillan, 1944), p. 212.

stand his teaching, both ethical and physical, we must bear in mind the concerns of a humanitarian in the world of fear described by Fustel de Coulanges: neither good will nor the exact performance of rites give complete assurance against the dark forces in control of human destiny.[5] Men crippled by the expectation of never-ending misfortune need a world vision which removes the fear of death, the fear of the gods, and the fear of fate. The physical system of Democritus fulfills part of this program. In a theory of atomistic materialism, the soul is but the most subtle part of the body. A set of particularly smooth and swift-moving atoms, it scatters when death comes, and the prospect of painless inexistence dismisses worries about another life. The fear of the gods is easily remedied by the picture of a separate world where man-like persons of imperishable essence carry on a life of enjoyment untroubled by whatever happens here below. But the physics of Democritus involves a theory of necessity which might increase, rather than alleviate, the fear of fate. In the words of Epicurus

> . . . it were better to follow the myths about the gods than to become a slave to the destiny of the natural philosophers: for the former suggests a hope of

[5] *The Ancient City*, Bk. I.

placating the gods by worship, whereas the latter involves a necessity which knows no placation.[6]

Democritean physics had to be modified on the subject of necessity. Epicurus conceives the world as made of unlimited empty space and of infinitely many atoms, falling like drops of rain in parallel lines. By itself, this construct says that things happen according to predetermined patterns and inflexible directions. In order that the fear of fate be removed, events must be allowed some flexibility. The implacable picture of fall along vertical paths must be softened by unpredictable deviations. What Lucretius calls *clinamen,* swerve, is the atom's ability to deviate, unpredictably and uncausally, from the straight line. These deviations play an essential role in the genesis of worlds inasmuch as they account for the formation of aggregates.[7] If

[6] "Letter to Menoeceus," translated by C. Bailey in *The Stoic and Epicurean Philosophers* (New York: Random House, 1940), p. 33.

[7] It seems that in Democritus atoms move, by strict necessity, in all directions; their movement is considered indistinct from their essence and therefore calls for no explanation: the formation of aggregates raises no particular problem. According to another interpretation, the atoms of Democritus fall vertically, but the heavier ones move at greater speed than the lighter ones, and this

atoms moved along parallels, how would they gather into bodies? But more importantly the swerve is the principle of contingency and free choice. Lucretius says:

Once again, if every motion is always linked on, and the new always arises from the old in order determined, nor by swerving do the first-beginnings [*primordia*] make a certain start of movement to break through the decrees of fate, so that cause may not follow cause from infinite time; whence comes this free will for living things all over the earth; whence, I ask, is it wrested from fate, this will whereby we move forward, where pleasure leads each one of us, and swerve likewise in our motions neither at determined times nor in a determined direction of place, but just where our mind has carried us? For without doubt it is his own will which gives to each one a start for this movement, and from the will the motions pass flooding through the limbs. . . . Wherefore in the seeds too you must needs allow likewise that there is another

---

would account for collisions and the constitution of aggregates. Epicurus holds, on the contrary, that in a vacuum all bodies fall at an identical speed, so that a difference of weight cannot produce a collision. Whether Epicurus differs from Democritus with regard to the direction of atomic movements, or only with regard to the relative speed of falling atoms, his world picture, so long as the swerve theory has not been brought in, expresses the idea of universal necessity in a more simple and convincing manner than that of Democritus.

> cause of motion besides blows and weights, whence comes this power born in us, since we see that nothing can come to pass from nothing. For weight prevents all things coming to pass by blows, as by some force without. But that the very mind feels not some necessity within it doing all things, and is not constrained like a conquered thing to bear and suffer, this is brought about by the tiny swerve of the first-beginnings in no determined direction of place and at no determined time.[8]

The swerve is imperceptible to the sense and consequently cannot be denied by any experience (Lucretius, *op. cit.*, Bk. II, lines 249–250). Here is an example of what has been called the rule of noninvalidation [οὐκ ἀντιμαρτύρησις], a special feature of Epicurean logic. The Epicurean sometimes seems to hold a proposition sufficiently established by the fact that no experience can prove it false. The physics of Epicurus is a hypothetical and deductive system finally vindicated, in terms of absolute truth, by its moral adequacy. Whereas a pure physicist may be satisfied with constructions from which observable regularities can be logically derived, the Epicurean philosopher needs constructs which not only infer physical phenomena but also bear out definite insights on the good life of man. If the atomism of

[8] *On the Nature of Things*, trans. Cyril Bailey (Oxford: Clarendon Press, 1947), Bk. II, lines 251–293.

Democritus, modified by the theory of the swerve, satisfies the demands of moral life without conflicting with any data of physical experience, it is a successful hypothesis, and the uniqueness of its success finally establishes its truth. For the relevant consequences inferred by this system cannot be derived from any other system.

In order to understand in what sense the swerve involves a denial of causality, let its description be compared with the causelessness attributed to a chance event in those systems which acknowledge the reality of chance. For Aristotle as well as for Cournot, some events are constituted merely by the encounter of two or more unrelated causal processes. Of any such event it can be said with complete appropriateness that it has no cause, for it does not have any cause in an essential sense. It has causes, indeed, but because their plurality is not unified, all its causes are accidental. The causelessness of the swerve is more radical than that of a chance occurrence. What happens by chance results from causes, even though it has no essential cause. But the swerve has neither cause nor causes. Its description sharply contrasts with that of the chance event since, far from taking place at the point where causal lines meet, it is designed to bring about a possibility of collision among lines which, otherwise, would remain indefinitely parallel. The accidental and fortuitous happenings described by Aristotle are grounded in natural necessity. The nonessential encounter of two causal processes presupposes the essential definiteness of these processes. But the Epicurean swerve is a thing contingent in an absolute sense. It springs from nowhere and holds natural necessity in check.[9] With regard to the theory of freedom, Epicureanism enjoys a unique significance inasmuch as it places the principle of all free choice in an act of contingency boldly conceived apart from any cause, any nature, and any intelligible ground.[10]

[9] ". . . this deviation takes place spontaneously at a time and in a place that are completely indetermined, since it is without a cause" (Bréhier, *Histoire de la Philosophie* [Presses Universitaires de France, 1945], Vol. 1, p. 347).

[10] [Prof. Simon frequently referred to Epicureanism and to the theory of the swerve because it seemed to him to exemplify clearly and purely the notion that freedom from necessity required an absence—an interruption—of causality. It thus provided an almost perfect contrast to his own view that freedom is to be found not along the line of causelessness but along the line of causality. See for example his exposition of Epicureanism in the brief section "Free Choice" in *The Tradition of Natural Law*, ed. by Vukan Kuic (New York: Fordham University Press, 1965), pp. 58–60. The same point is made at greater length in a tape recording of a lecture in Professor Simon's course "The Matter and Form of Morality" (ca. 1954) at

This interpretation of freedom in terms of radical contingency combines with a materialistic system of explanation. Let us remove from our minds the polemical connotations often associated with the word "materialism" and its derivatives, and let us bracket all that can be said for or against materialism in terms of aesthetic and morality. Let us also disregard, as irrelevant for the present discussion, the negation of spiritual substance. Materialism is best defined by the set purpose of giving precedence to explanations through material causes. Indeed, there is nothing materialistic about vividly realizing the significance of material causality in nature, in human affairs, in metaphysics, and in logic. What characterizes the materialistic spirit is a stubborn resolution to use material causes regardless of the cost, i.e., even when parsimony points to causes of another order. Consider a situation whose objective features do not, by any means, rule out an explanation through causes other than material, and suppose that the line of material causality is followed —without discussion or vindication: clearly it is assumed that no explanation is valid unless it proceeds from material causes. This assumption epitomizes the spirit of materialism. The Epicureans

the Committee on Social Thought, the University of Chicago. Ed.]

disregard without examination or mention the theory that the principle of freedom should be sought on the level of wholes and organisms rather than on the level of elements. They take for granted that freedom, if there is such a thing, must derive from the primary components of things. In the interpretation of materialism, it often happens that the significant relation is not so much that of body to spirit as that of part to whole. The parts are the material cause of the whole. Starting from our experience of free choice it can be reasonably wondered whether the principle of choice should be considered a property of the atom or a property of the thing, viz. man, described as an aggregate of atoms. For the Epicureans freedom would not exist at all if its principle did not exist on the atomic level. No arrangement of atoms will ever break Democritean necessity unless the individual component of aggregates can deviate from the straight line. This search for freedom in the realm of the part, of the ultimate part, of the elementary component of things, is one of the everlasting representative traits of Epicureanism. When modern physicists came to attribute to the behavior of particles a character of indeterminacy,[11] men of

[11] ["In 1927 Heisenberg set in motion a new development in the quantum theory and the consequences were

science, philosophers, and cultured readers alike felt that freedom was at last given a chance. A. S. Eddington suggested humorously that, though for a physicist it never had made sense until 1927, it was making sense for the first time.[12] In classical mechanics the path of every particle was strictly determined; there was no room for choice in a world where elementary processes followed lines subject to increasingly precise calculation. For the problem of freedom to make sense, determinism had to be challenged in the pathways of the primary particles. *Yet there is nothing obviously absurd about relating freedom to forms, wholes, and organisms rather than to primary components.*

The use of a materialistic method in the search for freedom begs the question of freedom's nature. If freedom is, by set purpose, sought on the material side of things; if freedom is basically conceived after the pattern of material properties; if freedom is intelligibly traced to the material properties; if

---

further elaborated by Bohr. The outcome of it is a fundamental general principle which seems to rank in importance with the principle of relativity. I shall here call it the '*principle of indeterminacy*.' The gist of it can be stated as follows: *a particle may have position or it may have velocity but it cannot in any exact sense have both*" (Eddington, *The Nature of the Physical World* [New York: Macmillan, 1927], p. 220). Ed.]

[12] *Ibid.*, p. 350.

freedom is intelligibly traced to the material cause of things, to "that out of which" things are made, freedom is necessarily conceived as *in*determination, absence of determination, formlessness, causelessness, groundlessness, and irrationality. The swerve of the Epicureans is the uninhibited expression of a philosophy that we shall recognize whenever freedom or its principle is sought on the part of the material cause.

Let it be remarked that the forcible use of material causality is not found only in the systems which reject noncorporeal substance. In the spirit also there is room for the relation between whole and parts and between the more primitive and the more completely formed. The images of disorder described at the beginning of this chapter are products of materialistic imagination—a well-known companion of common sense, which we are not surprised to see at work in the treatment of a question which was treated by common sense before philosophers had a chance to say anything about it. All would be relatively simple if materialistic interpretations played their role in theories about bodies alone. But in the spirit also there is such a thing as a material side of things and, within systems never described as materialistic, freedom happens to be interpreted as a *clinamen* of spiritual motions.

2

The Will

VOLUNTARINESS

IMAGES OF DISORDER and the notion of independence from external forces combine in some paradoxical remarks of Philip Frank on the subject of freedom. The best approximation to complete freedom is found in a person who, "while deeply engaged in the course of his ideas, suddenly elicits an act . . . suggested by an association, or by an image springing from his unconscious." Frank remarks, further, that "something of the same kind occurs in certain cases of insanity, in which acts are very little influenced by external circumstances."[1] Yet many would not hesitate to say that these are typical examples of involuntary acts, and hold it unacceptably paradoxical to describe them as distinguished approximations to complete freedom. To be sure, of all the grounds that can be tentatively assigned to freedom, voluntariness is the most obviously suggested by experience. Let us, accordingly, compare two acts outwardly similar, of which one, however, is considered by common interpretation of experience to be voluntary, and the other one involuntary. Such a comparative description should bring forth the distinguishing features of the voluntary act and make it possible to decide whether voluntariness constitutes a ground for freedom.

Here are some homely examples. A motorist is driving on a winding and dangerous road. He has been driving for several hours; he is tired and drowsy. He made a mistake in not stopping at the last town for a rest and a cup of coffee. Now he must go on in spite of fatigue. Suddenly a beautiful dog steps onto the roadway a few feet ahead of the car. It is too late to stop, and on the left side another

[1] *Das Kausalgesetz und seine Grenzen* (Vienna: Springer, 1932), p. 150.

car is approaching at high speed. The driver turns right and the car falls into a ravine. He survives.

In the same setting another driver perceives at a distance a group of children walking on the shoulder of the road. They are safe and there is no reason why he should slow down. But one of the children drops a rubber ball which rolls across the roadway. The child runs after the ball. In a split second the driver realizes the situation. Sometimes it does not take much time to achieve perfect attention and go through a complete deliberation. It is too late to stop and on the left side a car is approaching fast. The driver must run over the child or expose himself to almost certain death. He crashes into the ravine but survives.

In the hospital the two men owe some explanations to their friends and relatives. The first confesses that he did not act reasonably, but he does not like to be blamed for having acted absurdly. True, he was unreasonable an hour earlier when he needed a rest but yielded to his desire to get home, and drove on. To the question: "Did you really mean to lay down your life in order to save that of the dog?" he answers that he did not mean anything. He did not act for a purpose. He would like to say that he did not *act* at all but rather *was driven*—precisely the thing which should never happen to a driver. He did not ask what was the greater good. He did not think of the better and the worse. He was nearly napping. He did not know where he was going. He did not know what he was doing. He felt that this beautiful animal should not be run over. He just saw the dog and turned the wheel.

No matter how modest, the second driver must confess that he knew where he was going and what he was doing when he boldly exposed his life to preserve that of a child. He was not drowsy, he was awake and attentive, and very much aware of what was happening. It did not take him more than a very small fraction of a second to realize that he had to choose between going to an almost certain death, or being for the rest of his life the man who had run over a child. He was not eager to die, but the prospect of this horror seemed to him unacceptable: every day and night, perhaps for half a century and more, to be a man who, in order not to die, consented to be instrumental in a child's death. It was too much and he felt that he hated the death of a child more than his own death. He was as fond of life as any sound and hopeful young man; but under the circumstances he simply found it good to go to death. Saving the child at the cost of his own life was what he considered good under circumstances that he had not chosen. The facts being what they were, it was good to drive into the ravine.

The conduct of the second driver exemplifies ethical excellence: here is a man who voluntarily does what is morally good—nay, delivers himself to the requirements of heroic perfection. In this example the excellence of virtue served to emphasize the voluntariness of action, but voluntariness may be found also, and no less certainly, in a course of action morally inferior or definitely bad. If the question concerns voluntariness as opposed to involuntariness, the consideration of virtue and vice is altogether accidental. The voluntary action is essentially relative to the good, but not necessarily to what is morally good. In any situation I may find it good to observe the rule of morality but I may, just as well, find it good to procure an advantage incompatible with this rule. What matters is the connection between my action and my judgment that it is good, for some reason or other, to elicit this action. The first driver did not act voluntarily because he was too drowsy to do such a thing as to see the good, to recognize the good, to place the good in one thing or in another, in action or in abstention. He feels that his friends should not ask him whether he really meant to sacrifice his life for a dog: this question ignores the circumstances of his drowsiness. He saw the dog and turned the wheel, and that is all there is to the story. He never thought that it was good to lay down his life for a dog. He was too tired to think. If his power of thinking had not been suspended, he certainly would have found it good to save his life, he would have placed the good in the preservation of his own life. He does not want to be blamed or teased for an action altogether involuntary. Rather, he would accept the blame for not having stopped and rested when he felt that uninterrupted driving involved an absurd danger. It takes some will power to stop a car when you are far from your home, and still more when you are close to it. He was too lazy to stop. His laziness made him find it good to keep going, although he knew that he was acting unreasonably.

As to the man confronted by the risk of running over a child, he may, as in our story, judge that it is good to sacrifice his own life. He may just as well consider that it is good to remain alive regardless of what happens to a child who, after all, was not supposed to be playing on the roadway. There also may be in the back seat a person whose life must be preserved, for the sake of the common good, even at the cost of a very painful sacrifice. The driver on the winding road may be responsible for the commander in chief of an army engaged in just action, or for half a dozen children entrusted to his care: in either case he would rightly judge that it is good, under the circumstances, not to drive into the ravine.

The good to which voluntary action is relative is not restricted to the genus of morality or to any other genus. It is not particular in any sense whatsoever. It is *the* nonparticular good. It transcends all its embodiments and, though engaged in every thing that is good, it is not circumscribed by any of the things in which it is embodied. It is at work, so to say, in all pursuits and all enjoyments. It is immense, it is present in rest and in motion, in contemplation and in action, in study and in business, in pleasure and in austerity, in the gratifications of the senses and in those of the spirit, in the ways of justice and in those of crime. It is present in revolt and blasphemy, in the delight of breaking the law, of doing wrong with full awareness of the right and the wrong. It has the character of a form with regard to all the particular things or actions in which it is realized.

To designate the good, considered as form of all the things good and as the distinguishing object of the will, St. Thomas and his followers use the words *bonum in communi*. This expression will be easily misunderstood unless it is firmly set in opposition to *bonum in particulari*; it is merely designed to bring forth the nonparticularity of the good regarded by voluntary actions, its inexhaustible ability to transcend the things in which it materializes. Let the words *in communi* never be allowed to bring into the picture conditions of abstraction—worst of all, conditions of univocal abstraction—which would sharply conflict with the nature of volition and, more generally, with that of appetition. Such phrases as "the good so understood as to comprehend all goods" or "the all-embracing nature of the good" would convey rather exactly the meaning of *bonum in communi*. The expression "the comprehensive good" can be used as a substitute for these heavy phrases.[2]

[2] None of this means that the will desires abstract qualities. We call "money-minded" an individual who takes no interest in things and persons except *insofar* as they procure money for him. Everything which he desires he desires under the aspect of being financially interesting. We could say without impropriety that what he loves is "being financially interesting": this includes all enterprises which relate to it and transcends each one of them. Nevertheless, the money-minded man is not suspected of being passionate about formal abstract causes: he wants very concrete things by reason of their participation in the universal essence of being financially interesting. In the same way, the will desires the good which transcends all particular goods and desires concrete things by reason of their participation in the universal essence of good.

On account of its amplitude the comprehensive good does not admit of a definition properly so called, but a valuable substitute for a definition can be obtained by considering its relations to infinity.

The comprehensive good is not determinately finite; yet it cannot be identified with the infinite good. A good determinately infinite cannot exist in combination with any evil, or with any limitation of goodness. The comprehensive good does *admit of* coincidence with the infinite good; it should be said that the climax of its intelligibility is attained in such coincidence. Likewise, the concept of being exercises the fullness of its energy when it comes to signify being without privation or limitation—the unreceived and unrestricted act of to be. But just as the common concept of being admits of limited realizations and excludes no limitation—it excludes only contradiction, which would annihilate it—so the comprehensive good excludes no conceivable limitation of goodness: it admits of all the limitations that it transcends and excludes only the fiction of an evil subsisting by itself. The comprehensive good is embodied in the most particular objects of desire, e.g. in the short-lived sweetness of vengeance obtained at the cost of hideous felony. But any particular thing in which it is embodied fails, by an infinite distance, to coincide with it. In short, the infinity of the comprehensive good is that of a form which admits of existence in particular bearers, but whose power cannot be exhausted by any bearer distinct from itself. As a form, as an act, as an energy, the comprehensive good is infinite; but, by reason of its very comprehensiveness, it admits of existing in subjects inadequate to its infinity. When there is adequacy between the good thing and the comprehensive good itself, the good thing is no longer good in one respect and evil in another, good at one time and not at another. Goodness is no longer subject to growth and decay. The good thing no longer has the character of a bearer distinct from the form that it bears. Goodness subsists by itself as a concrete infinity. What Plato said of the relation between a transcendent form and its infinite existence in the case of the beautiful applies clearly to the good.

> He who has been instructed thus far in the things of love, and who has learned to see the beautiful in due order and succession, when he comes toward the end will suddenly perceive a nature of wondrous beauty (and this, Socrates, is the final cause of all our former toils)—a nature which in the first place is everlasting, not growing and decaying, or waxing and waning; secondly, not fair in one point of view and foul in another, or at one time or in one relation or at one place fair, at another time or in another relation

or at another place foul, as if fair to some and foul to others, or in the likeness of a face or hands or any other part of the bodily frame, or in any form of speech or knowledge, or existing in any other being, as for example in an animal, or in heaven, or in earth, or in any other place; but beauty absolute, separate, simple, and everlasting, which without diminution and without increase, or any change, is imparted to the ever-growing and perishing beauties of all other things.[3]

Substitute, in this description, the good for the beautiful. Assume, further, that contemplation is both intuitive and intelligent. Adherence to the comprehensive good intuitively and intelligently grasped is the most voluntary, the least constrained, the least coerced, the most spontaneous of all actions. Yet this supremely voluntary action involves no choice and accordingly no freedom. Choice is between something and something else, namely, between acting and non-acting. Philosophers may never be in a position to decide whether an intuition of the comprehensive good is possible at all for a finite intellect. But a proposition whose truth can be philosophically established is the conditional: "If there is an intuition of the comprehensive good there is also determinate adherence to it" in spontaneity, in voluntariness and without choice. Be-

[3] *Symposium*, trans. B. Jowett, 210E–211B.

tween what and what would there be choice? Not between a good and its opposite, for there is no opposition within the good which is not "existing in any other being . . . but . . . [is] absolute, separate, simple and everlasting," and not between "to adhere" and "not to adhere," for, if the good contemplated is absolute and the contemplation intuitive, adhering is perceived as altogether desirable and nonadhering is devoid of any object. Thus, whereas voluntariness seems to be the ground of free choice, it is not purely and simply identifiable with free choice. In one case at least—but a distinguished one, even though it may remain for the philosopher entirely hypothetical—there is unqualified voluntariness without freedom.

The difficulties in which we are now engaged call for an inquiry into the nature and the natural inclination of the will: this is our best chance to understand the decisively significant relation between mere freedom from constraint and free choice. Whatever is natural is free from constraint. Again, whatever is voluntary is free in a better sense, free from constraint. The problem is whether the nature which transcends the natural way of acting by achieving the distinguished spontaneity of voluntariness also transcends the common pattern of natural causation by achieving freedom from necessity.

THE PASSIONS OF MAN

The nonvoluntary way of reacting, which was exemplified in the preceding section by the disastrous movement of the sleepy driver who felt that he could not run over a dog, admits of extreme diversity. Human reactions opposed to voluntariness are usually called, with much imprecision, by such words as tropisms, reflexes, instinctive drives, physical pleasures and pains, feelings of tension and relaxation, feelings of stimulation and depression, needs, tendencies, inclinations, leanings, affections, efforts, emotions, passions, dispositions, and complexes. Let us call "emotional sphere" the whole set of such reactions.

According to all sensationist doctrines, the emotional system constitutes the entirety of human desire, and the word "will," if still used at all, designates a thing that can be reduced to some component of emotional life. Whether the will exists as a distinct power of appetition is a question of truly fundamental significance in the theory of freedom. Many systems ignore it, but it is impossible not to suspect that such ignorance has something to do with the shortcomings which commonly impair philosophic discourse on freedom: uncritical submission to images and to confused analogies; the crippling influence of unexamined and unformulated postulates concerning determinism, causality, spontaneity, order, intelligibility, and contingency; and the failure to ascertain the real meaning of the suggestions which come from our moral sentiments.

At the present stage of our inquiry the meaning of the word "will" is not totally unspecified. The preceding description of reactions commonly described as voluntary or involuntary supplies all the advantages of a nominal and dialectical definition, even though it seems neither necessary nor helpful to sum up this description in the conventional style of definitory formulas. We know what we are looking for as we state the question: besides all the powers involved in what we call the emotional systems, is there in man a power of distinct nature, definable in relation to the features which distinguish the voluntary from the involuntary acts? If such a power exists, it is likely to modify human emotions and to reveal its existence within the emotional system itself.

Consider a group of tendencies relative to such biological purposes as nutrition and reproduction. The object of these tendencies is not only finite but also contained within narrow limits. True, the behavior of animals contains traits of luxury and lavishness; it admits of trials and errors, losses, failures, and disorder. Instinct does not assure a strict adjustment of desire to the ends of animal life. "The bird sings much more than it is allowed to by the Darwinian theory of sexual selection." [4] It sings much more than the preservation of the species demands. But it does not sing to infinity, to exhaustion and to death. In animals, luxury and disorder do not have the character of a devouring frenzy, save perhaps in a small number of cases. In man, on the contrary, biological desires, as soon as they are not controlled by the virtuous reason, expand indefinitely, become frantic, miss their object and destroy their subject. If such facts of furious destruction are relatively rare, it is because the conditions upon which they depend are seldom realized. Few men succeed in destroying completely the structure of rational rules built in their souls by religion and society. Let it be said that insofar as the rules of the virtuous reason are lacking, frenzy gets hold of desires. This does not happen only as an exception but constantly. Every rebel bears witness to the destructive infinity of emancipated desires.

Let us make clear the paradox contained in these

[4] Frederik J. Buytendijk, "Les différences essentielles des fonctions psychiques de l'homme et des animaux" in *Vue sur la psychologie animale* (Paris: Vrin, 1930), p. 76.

familiar facts. The rules of action resulting from biological structure and animal instinct should, if all things were equal, suffice to assure the government of man in his animal life; but, plainly, they do not. A purely sensible desire would be a matter proportionate to the forms of instinct; but the matter that instinct vainly endeavors to control is a desire animated, agitated, tormented, expanded and sometimes devastated by the quest for infinity which is characteristic of the spirit. Spiritual activities are constantly at work inside the inferior activities which they animate and vitally pervade. If we were allowed to behave as pure animals, we would never be tempted to confuse understanding with sense apprehension, for an easy comparison would evince a striking contrast. But the comparision is not easy, for no purely animal sensation is present in our experience.

All our perceptions are human and pervaded with intellectuality. I try to experience a universe of forms and colors and I see only things that bear an intelligible sense: houses and gardens, people who come and go, a post office, a power plant. I cannot achieve the abstraction in reverse which would isolate these variegated spots from the complex and highly elaborated concepts which structure them in my perception. When we compare sense cognition with understanding, what we are actually considering, under the name of sense cognition, is a psychological composite from which it has been impossible to eliminate the intellectual component. Because the contrast is not sharp enough, the sensationistic reduction looks somewhat plausible.

Likewise, when we compare sense desires with appetitions born of understanding, what we apprehend as sense desire is a system from which understanding is not absent. The comparison is not actually between the rational appetite and the sense desire, but rather between an act of rational appetition incompletely isolated from concomitant emotions and an act of sense desire in which the act of rational appetition is secretly present. The vigor of the spirit, its ability to spread its energy in all parts of the human being, is what accounts for the appearances of which sensationist psychology takes advantage.

Let us call exasperation the process in which emotions and passions, through their indefinite amplitude, disclose the infinite nature of the will and of an energy capable of all the good. Under the name of Dionysian emotions Nietzsche describes a sublime form of exasperation. A delirium shaken by the shivers of sacred awe is brought about by the inebriation of the senses. How could this be, if there were not, within inebriation, an appetite capable of finding its joy in the metaphysical attributes of being? Universal harmony, superabundance, common and unanimous life, liberty, peace, the original unity rejoined at the cost of an immense negation of the distinction of forms, mystery and joy invading the entire soul: all these metaphysical marvels come forward at the call of spring, under the influence of fermented drinks, of dance and strident sounds, through emotions expressive of a love greater than the world and capable of the absolute.

Many contemporary writers have tried on themselves the effects of exasperation.[5] Among their ex-

[5] [Artists have been partial to "exasperation" in order to stimulate their imagination, to secure additional imagery, or to bring forth symbolic forms readily. In the contemporary context, one thinks immediately of those who use "mind-expanding" or hallucinogenic drugs in order to engender such a state. Professor Simon, however, no doubt had in mind such writers as De Quincey, Baudelaire, Rimbaud (see below), and Cocteau. In a note he also indicates that Nietzsche belongs in this group.

Nietzsche's metaphysics is grounded in pessimism and is partial to the artist and to "earnestness of life." In such a setting, Apollinian rapture—"that state of rapt repose in the presence of a visionary world, in the presence of *beautiful appearance* designed as a deliverance from *becoming*"—is illusory (*Complete Works of Friedrich Nietzsche*, ed. Oscar Levy [New York: Russell and Russell, 1964]; Introduction by E. Foerster-Nietzsche. Vol. I, *The*

periences that of Arthur Rimbaud is distinguished by a fierce determination in the fulfillment of a lucidly conceived scheme. The development of Rimbaud's genius is marked by an ever-more-intense and pervading delirium. A *Season in Hell* is the masterpiece of hallucinatory poetry.

Delirium implies the impairment of rational control and of adjustment to life. But the weakening of higher faculties, which releases imagination, may result either from a mere failure or from an active pursuit. When inhibition is merely undergone [passively], the products of imagination are poor things: they can hardly attain the dignity of the work of art; like the dreams of a sick man, they

---

Birth of Tragedy, translated by Wm. A. Haussman, p. xxv). "The muses of the arts of 'appearance' paled before an art which, in its intoxication, spoke the truth; the wisdom of Silenus cried 'woe! woe!' against the cheerful Olympians. The individual, with all its boundaries and due proportions, went under in the self-oblivion of the Dionysian states" (*ibid.*, p. 41).

Professor Simon also refers to Ruth Benedict, who in *Patterns of Culture* (Boston: Houghton Mifflin, 1934 [new ed., 1961]) maintains that the Plains Indians distinguish themselves as an Apollinian culture, apart from other American Indians, by their utilitarian or ceremonial handling of practices which are used by other cultures in a Dionysian fashion (See *op. cit.*, pp. 71ff.). Ed.]

are wanting in life. The poetic hallucinations of Rimbaud proceed from an active inhibition of the higher powers. The hallucinatory state in which his poetic experience is achieved and expressed is consciously striven at, and obtained at the cost of gigantic efforts and bitter remorse. "I could not continue, I would have become insane; further . . . it was wrong." We are not certain that Rimbaud actually uttered, just before his death, these words reported by his sister. Yet, these words convey exactly the situation of the poet in 1873 and contain a plausible explanation of his paradoxical farewell to poetry. It is easy to understand that two years of a delirium procured through active tension made him realize the imminent threat of insanity and caused him to suffer from an unbearable sense of guilt. But because he had chosen delirium as the instrument of his poetic experience, it was impossible to end his delirium without giving up poetry.

In Rimbaud the disorder of imagination and emotions proceeds from an excess of ambitious vitality, from the irresistible vehemence of a desire. Concerning the object of this desire, much information can be derived from *A Season in Hell* and from the two celebrated letters of May 1871.

Ah, I am so utterly forsaken that to any divine

image whatsoever, I offer my impulses toward perfection.[6]

Finally I came to regard as sacred the disorder of my mind.[7]

Meanwhile I debauch myself as much as possible. Why? I want to be a poet and I work at making myself *seeing*. . . . It is a matter of arriving at the unknown by the disordering of *all the senses.*[8]

The Poet makes himself *seeing* by a long, immense, and reasoned disordering of *all the senses.* All the forms of love, of suffering, of folly he experiences by himself. He himself is the filter to extract the quintessences of all poisons. Ineffable torture in which he needs all of faith, all of superhuman power, where he becomes the greatest sick person, the greatest criminal, the greatest evil-doer—and the supremely wise person! —for he arrives at the unknown! Because he has cultivated his soul, already rich, more than anyone else! He arrives at the unknown; and when, maddened, he would finally lose the understanding of his visions, he has seen them! Oh, that he would burst in his bonds by unheard-of and innumerable things. . . .[9]

[6] A *Season in Hell*, translated by Louise Varèse (New York: New Directions, 1961), "Bad Blood," p. 15.

[7] *Ibid.*, "Delirium. II. Alchemy of the Word," p. 55.

[8] To Georges Izambard, May 13, 1871, in "Lettres de la vie littéraire d'Arthur Rimbaud (1870–1875)," *réunies et annotées* by Jean-Marie Carré, *Nouvelle Revue Française* (1931), p. 55. Translated here by Paule Simon.

[9] To Paul Demeny, May 15, 1871, *ibid.*, p. 62.

The boundless force which gives birth to those enterprises of the poet is the spiritual will in the highest of its functions, the aspiration to mystical experience, the aspiration to an experimental union with the absolute. We know that mystical aspiration, if it is not to fall short of its object, must disengage itself from the senses and attain, through the ascetic way, to the full freedom of spiritual life. A supreme case of exasperation, the sacred delirium of Rimbaud is the product of an aberrant mystical aspiration which returns into the sensuous sphere and causes within it bewildering explosions.

Signs of the will can also be found in a phenomenon from which contemporary sensationism has derived very popular arguments. The sensationist interpretation of *sublimation*, widely distributed by countless popularizers, has done much to spread the belief that all that is lofty in our affective life is but a play of masks, a ridiculous or monstrous comedy played by our pride at the expense of our sincerity. If only an act of sincerity tears away the mask, he who used to consider himself an uncompromising servant of justice, a sincerely religious person, a born soldier, a lover of beauty, finds in himself nothing else but carnal desires and sexual perversion.

Let us try to put together a precise definition of

sublimation. As a research hypothesis it can be assumed that the sex drive, in its primitive phases, includes secondary components normally bound to disappear into the main component. If the main component is repressed, the instinctive impulse is driven into a side way and some secondary component expands instead of decreasing. A perverse tendency has begun to grow. Suppose that this tendency is itself repressed. Two cases are possible: sometimes instinctive energy is spent producing neurotic symptoms, and sometimes it finds an outlet in intellectual, artistic, social or religious activities. This advantageous channeling of sexual energy is what is called sublimation.

The concept of sublimation was soon given a wider sense. McDougall suggests that it should be applied not only to sexual energy but also to all forms of instinctive energy.

> Sublimation then becomes a word we may use to denote all instances in which instinctive energy or *hormé* or *libido* (in Jung's sense of the word) sustains activities which are higher (either in the intellectual or the moral sense) than purely instinctive activities.[10]

Let it be added, in philosophic terms, that the fact of sublimation, which seems to be perfectly estab-

[10] W. McDougall, *Outline of Abnormal Psychology* (New York: Scribner's, 1926), p. 473.

lished, evidences a causal continuity between instinctive tendencies and higher activities. That sexual appetites and other animal desires can be, under certain circumstances and in a certain way, the cause of such rational products as art, science, and social action seems to be established by experience. Possessed as they generally are with a Mephistophelic spirit of vilification, the Freudians could not help taking advantage of such a causal continuity against what is most human in man. Roland Dalbiez writes:

> The Freudian school is oriented in the direction of radical empiricism. . . . The conditioning of superior psychic apparatus by inferior psychic apparatus, translated into empirical language, becomes the reduction of reason to sense. The point of destination cannot really be superior to the point of departure. At bottom, for Freudians, sublimation is only a disguise of sexuality.[11]

But this is merely dodging the problem. All the difficulty arises indeed from the fact that the point of arrival is really superior to the point of departure and the rational effect really superior to the sensuous cause. Dalbiez writes further:

[11] Roland Dalbiez, *La méthode psychanalytique et la doctrine freudienne* (Paris: Desclée, 1936), Vol. I, p. 595.

> The principle of sufficient reason demands that the perfection of the effect be not greater than that of the cause. From this we must conclude that sexuality is not the proper cause of art. However important the role of the sexual instinct may be in aesthetic intuition, it is an accidental, not an essential, one.[12]

Thus the causal relation involved in the process of sublimation would be one of accidental causality. This interpretation seems insufficient, for facts of sublimation manifest with regularity a resemblance between the higher activity at the point of arrival and the lower appetite at the point of departure. Without this resemblance, the concept of sublimation would make no sense. Yet, one characteristic of the accidental cause is that it bears no resemblance to its effect. To use Aristotle's example, it may happen that a physician is also a singer. Then it can be said truthfully that a singer is responsible for the healing of a disease. Such a proposition surprises and sounds comic, because it brings forth an accidental causality and a striking absence of resemblance where a relation of essential causality and some sort of resemblance were expected. There is no resemblance between the intelligible features which make up the healing of a disease and those which define the singer. However, between the art

[12] *Ibid.*, Vol. II, p. 456.

of the physician and the healing of disease the resemblance is obvious.

The argument of Dalbiez contains an ambiguity. "The principle of sufficient reason [I would prefer to say the principle of causality] demands that the perfection of the effect be not greater than that of the cause." This holds for the principal cause, but not for the instrumental cause. In its instrumental function, and by reason of the efficiency which traverses it without belonging to it, the instrument actually causes effects superior to what its nature and its own efficiency allow it to cause. Let it be said, further, that the superiority of the effect over the instrumental cause is not measured by any definite proportion. A brush is a poor thing; yet all that is found in the works of Leonardo da Vinci has been caused by the brush of Leonardo. If it is true that the instinctive tendencies are in some way the cause of rational activities and if the causality which they exert is something else than accidental, then we have here to do with a relation of instrumental causality.

This is what Pfister—in general a rather orthodox Freudian—seems to surmise, in a page rendered confused by the lack of adequate philosophic expressions:

> . . . we have no right to say that the sexual impulse has been turned towards art or religion, with the implication that art and religion are merely sexual functions. This would be as crude a view as if we were to say that the work of a Michelangelo is merely to be regarded as a contraction of the muscles of the arm; or as if, as I myself once phrased it, the performance of Beethoven's violin concerto were to be called "a vibration of catgut." What has happened is that the mental energy with which an elementary psychical process is charged has now become associated with another sort of activity of the intellect and the will.[13]

Thus the process of sublimation, contrary to the expectation of those who did so much to make it known, bears evidence ultimately to the distinctness and the autonomy of the will. Imagine that a screen hides the painter without hiding the canvas and the brush. We do not hesitate to infer that the brush acts as instrument of a cause equal to the effect. If the colors that are being assembled show the characteristics of a work of genius, we know that the brush is held by the hand of an artist of genius. The sublimation of sensuous appetites reveals the will, just as the products of the brush reveal the genius

[13] Oskar Pfister, *Love in Children and its Aberrations* (London and New York: Dodd, Mead, 1924), p. 292.

of the painter. As the result of sensuous activity we observe effects that the sense appetite cannot cause by itself: this is perfectly intelligible if the sense appetite acts as instrument of the will. Otherwise it is absurd. The screen conceals the presence and activity of the spirit. But we see the instrument and the work, and we appreciate the disproportion between the work and the instrument. In the instrument which produces such a work a spiritual desire is present.

HAPPINESS AND THE LAST END

The relation of voluntary life to the good has often been expressed in the more homely language of a desire for happiness. The proposition that all men seek happiness naturally and necessarily is common, in varying degrees of explicitness, to Platonists, Aristotelians, Stoics, Augustinians, Thomists, and Humanists. It seems to have been more challenged in the last two centuries than in any period of the past. "I do not strive toward my happiness," Zarathustra says, "I strive toward my work." [14] In trends of great

[14] "*Fellow-suffering! Fellow-suffering with the higher men!*" he cried out, and his countenance changed into brass. "Well! *That* hath had its time! My suffering and my fellow-suffering—what matter about them! Do I then strive after *happiness*? I strive after my work!

"Well! The lion hath come, my children are nigh, Zara-

moral significance, happiness seems to be replaced, as object of human striving, by the fulfillment of duty, the achievement of power, the control of man over nature, cultural refinement, etc. True, it makes sense to say that these substitutions do not reach the heart of the matter, and that whoever strives toward his work rather than his happiness has actually placed his happiness in his work. Yet anyone familiar with the social and historical significance of moral ideas would not perceive any redundance in the view that it is the distinction of humanistic civilizations to place happiness in happiness, the end of man in the happiness of man. We are here confronted by a contrast, both parts of which are certain in terms of moral experience. Of an artist who sacrifices his fortune, his health, his love, his honor, and his soul to his creation, it can be said relevantly that he has placed his happiness in his creation. But he can also relevantly reply that for the sake of his work, he has surrendered all claim to happiness. From the study of this contrast much can be learned

---

thustra hath grown ripe, mine hour hath come: This is *my* morning, *my* day beginneth: *arise now, arise* thou great noontide."

Thus spake Zarathustra, and left his cave, glowing and strong, like a morning sun coming out of gloomy mountains. [*Thus Spake Zarathustra, op. cit.*, Vol. XI, LXXX —"The Sign," pp. 401–402.]

about the meaning and conditions of harmony in human desire.

The happiness that all men desire by nature and necessity has the character of a form capable of inadequate embodiment in indefinitely many matters. Whatever satisfies a tendency is a thing in which the form of happiness can be placed. In this basic and transcendental sense, Zarathustra deceives himself as he cherishes the belief that he has overcome the common striving of men for happiness and replaced it by something more distinguished and sophisticated, such as the striving toward one's work.

But among the things in which happiness is actually placed by men, some unite harmoniously with the form of happiness and some behave as if they could not undergo this form without suffering some sort of violence. We do not only mean that there is such a thing as true happiness and such a thing as false happiness. We do not only mean that the form of happiness can be placed in the proper and in the wrong subject, according as order is observed or not in the accomplishment of human tendencies. Induction shows that things in harmonious relation to happiness are characterized by their agreement with nature, their interiority to man, their being enjoyable in peace and their being enjoyable in common. With regard to the first and most basic of these features, let it be said that contemporary literature presents striking examples of human attitudes held and cherished precisely because of their being at variance with nature. An artist who considers that the duty of art is to give the lie to nature and who has dedicated his own substance to an embodiment of his artistic ideal, would be very willing to say that he does not strive toward his happiness but rather toward his art. No doubt, he is deceiving himself, and his art is actually the thing in which he has placed his happiness. Yet, the contrast is meaningful, though not ultimate. It is possible indeed to place happiness in aversion to nature, but if we inquire into *true* happiness, into the thing in which the form of happiness demands to be placed, one of the very first features that we shall find, one of the features closest to the very form of happiness, is agreement with nature. The artist dedicated to giving nature the lie in his art, and in a life shaped after the pattern of a work of art, can indulge in some meaningful way the claim to be seeking not happiness but something else. This claim is made meaningful by the absence of one of the most formal features of the thing in which the form of happiness truly consents to reside. There is, or there can be, an order inside a material cause; among the components of a "bearer," one may be closer to, and the other more remote from, the form. What is, within a bearer, closer to the form has itself the character of a form in relation to more remote components. In short, when Zarathustra declares: "I do not strive toward my happiness, I strive toward my work," the proposition is rendered meaningful not by the absence of the form of happiness, but by the absence of one or several of the most formal features of the subject in which happiness can be placed truly.

To sum up: the proposition that all men want to be happy is not properly understood unless it refers to happiness in such a purely formal way as to be fully compatible with the extremely significant fact that many men are aware of seeking something else than happiness.

To understand properly the notion of happiness as the end of voluntary action, it is necessary, further, to bear in mind the relation between real achievement and pleasure. An organism in need of water attains a state of real achievement when its normal ratio of water is restored; if this organism is endowed with consciousness, the state of need is normally notified by a particular feeling and the state of real achievement normally causes the experience of pleasure. We call real achievement the state of affairs constituted by the union of a natural tendency with its object. Just as an organism endowed with intelligence naturally tends toward the possession of truth, and just as the satisfaction of a biological need procures a pleasure, so the satisfaction of the urge toward truth brings about the joy of knowing.

In our daily interpretation of happiness we sometimes refer to real achievement, and sometimes to pleasure and joy, and sometimes we refer unanalytically to the real achievement and to the pleasure that follows upon it. We say, for instance, that a man of lofty character is really happy in a situation marked by acute suffering.[15] Such language is readily understood, and yet it conveys a paradox. To say that the just is really happy in his suffering makes sense, inasmuch as justice is a real achievement of excellent rank; but inasmuch as there is suffering instead of joy, order is upset and the happiness of which we speak is but relative and qualified. We happen, on the other hand, to remark that some people find happiness in crime. We express ourselves, on such a subject, with significant hesitations; some would say that no one should worry about those people since they feel perfectly

[15] See for example Plato, *Gorgias*, 478D, and *Republic*, Bk. X, 613B.

happy; others would say that the greatest of all misfortunes is precisely the coincidence of evil and joy which, by suppressing the warnings of pain, dims the prospect of restoration to real goodness. Clearly, when evil and joy coincide, happiness is understood in a strongly qualified sense. Unqualified happiness, happiness properly so called, involves both real achievement and the pleasure or joy normally following upon it.

True, the separation of real achievement and pleasure, which is a matter of very common experience, raises a problem. If pleasure is a conscious effect of real achievement, it is hard to see how real achievement can be accompanied by a state of pain and how pleasure can accompany destruction. The problem would not arise, the normal concomitance of real achievements and pleasure would be realized with perfect regularity, if the human dynamism were not made of a multiplicity of tendencies. Such multiplicity involves a possibility of interference and entails a demand for order. Again, the problem would not arise if nature assured this order invariably; but, by obvious experience, this is not the case. Whenever a tendency is satisfied without the requirements of order being met, there is pleasure, by reason of accomplishment, and destruction by reason of disorder. Consider for instance the case of a man dedicated to a passion for learning: to this passion he sacrifices his wealth, his health, his social life, his most sacred duties, and his soul. He is not really happy, although he enjoys this kind of life. We say that he is not really happy because the sacrifices following upon his passion involve disorder and a destruction for his person considered as a whole. Yet his illusionary happiness results from a real achievement, viz., from the real perfection of his intellect, won at the cost of disorderly sacrifice.

Again, the satisfaction of any tendency in a pluralistic system such as the human dynamism demands balance, equilibrium, harmony, and a hierarchic distribution of accomplishments. It is important to distinguish, in this connection, what pertains to the essence of multitude and what pertains to the particular character of pluralistic dynamism in the case of man. Let it be said, roughly, that the demand for order pertains to the metaphysical nature of the multitude, whereas the need for sacrifice corresponds to the particularities of multitudinous dynamism in things natural and material. Any dynamic whole demands that order should obtain in the satisfaction of the tendencies which make it up; but it is not necessary that the satisfaction of one tendency should conflict with that of another; accordingly, it is not by metaphysical necessity that order involves sacrifice. Order comes to involve sacrifice when and only when there is some sort of contrariety among the tendencies which make up the whole, so that the satisfaction of one tendency—say, toward good health—is incompatible with that of another tendency—say, toward universal knowledge. The law of contrariety, i.e., of the incompatibility of forms, originates in matter and, within the complex unity of man, centers on material conditions; but the effect of these conditions extends to all parts and functions of human life.

At this point it is necessary to ask in what sense, or senses, the notion of happiness implies totality of satisfaction, plenitude of accomplishment and joy, the saturation of desire, and should be declared incompatible with any residuum of unsatisfied tendency. Let this question be divided into two phases. Consider, first, the total set of the tendencies which make up the human dynamism. To the question whether happiness implies the satisfaction of each and all of these tendencies, the answer obviously is in the affirmative. So long as something remains to be desired our happiness is qualified and from this it is readily inferred that the only happiness attainable in the connatural condition of the human nature is a strongly qualified happiness. Within this condition at least one component of happiness will be missing, viz., everlasting enjoyment. The antinomy involved in a so-called happiness doomed to termination and constantly threatened with violent extinction is an inexhaustible commonplace of human complaint.

This consideration of infinity in duration leads to the second phase of the question, which can be most clearly described by way of a contrast with the first. In the first phase, a set of desires is considered precisely as a set, i.e., as a whole made of members, and what matters is whether the concept of happiness allows any member of this set to be left unsatisfied. Let us now consider, with regard to amplitude and comprehensiveness, the objects of the desires which make up the human dynamism. What matters, in this connection, is whether the objects of human desires are contained within limits or extend to infinity. Let us consider here those desires which proceed from the rational grasp of the good and pertain to voluntary life. Clearly these desires extend in unlimited manner to the whole universe of being and its perfections.

Humanistic and humane studies disclose the restless heart described by St. Augustine. Exploration into the heart of man often leads to the discovery of God via the infinity of human desire. To put an end to this restlessness and force the human heart into the pattern of positivistic peace, Auguste Comte multiplied the warnings of his patronizing serenity against the ever recurring abuses of "idle curiosity." In consistent manner he was led to impose drastic restrictions on scientific progress, and soon he was obliged to isolate himself from what was going on in the contemporary scientific movement. Thus, the scientific movement of the nineteenth century would have quickly ended in failure if Comte had been taken seriously by physicists and mathematicians. Even in disciplines of a nonontological character, the spirit of science is driven by an eagerness which, through definite methods, regards an unlimited universe of truth. The infinite eagerness of the scientific spirit establishes, in spite of all valid boundaries, a sort of continuity between the positive sciences and the philosophy of human action, metaphysics and theology. Positivism is probably the most consistent effort ever made to hold in check the human urge toward infinite accomplishment. This effort was intelligently centered on the very source and soul of infinity in man, viz., the intellect, and on what is most firm and most ambitious in intellectual life, viz., science. The positivistic attempt has been and remains favored by a unique set of historical circumstances. Because of the location of positivism in the nature and in the history of the human mind, the adventures of positivism are extraordinarily informative. All aspects of resistance to positivism—in religion, in ethics, in art, in the interpretation of history, in metaphysics, in the philosophy of nature, in positive science itself, in industrial life, in medical and psychiatric technique—express an aspect of man's adherence to infinity.

The distinctive feature of the voluntary act, which has been described as a relation to the good and as a relation to happiness, can also be described, from a slightly different standpoint, as a relation to the final end. It is by the same constitutive necessity that every voluntary act involves adherence to the good, adherence to happiness, and adherence to the final end. The first description is properly relative to the independence, unconditionality, and transcendence of the good; in the second description, the good was considered in the capacity of happiness, i.e., in its ability to procure the total well-being of a rational nature. Again, let us now consider the good as the term of means and of anything that participates in the nature of the means.

Acts of men are related to a last end in proportion as they are rational. Recall the explanations given to friends and relatives by the driver who avoided hitting a dog by running into a ravine: his struggles to make them understand that he never decided to lay down his life *in order that* the life of a dog be preserved. If he had understood what the problem was, the dog would have been run over. There is indeed something obviously teleological about the behavior of a driver who sees a dog and turns the wheel; but such teleology pertains to nature and instinct, not to voluntariness. True, the character of a purpose attaches to the preservation of the life of a dog, but in rational discourse such a purpose is not allowed to act as if it were final. The drowsy motorist was a victim of the shortsightedness of instinct. Had he been more alert he would have looked beyond the good of protecting the life of a dog; this good would have been considered against the background of more basic purposes. Suppose that these are also of a nonterminal character; suppose, for instance that the nearly slumbering driver is a very ardent huntsman and that he is generous enough to think of how other huntsmen feel about their own dogs. In contrast to the case in the foregoing story, he did not just see the dog and turn the wheel; he saw the dog, recognized it as a pointer with a distinguished pedigree, thought of how sad and angry its owner would be, and then turned the wheel. Rationality goes on for part of the way, but irrationality soon gains control. In this new version of the case, the driver friendly to the dog's species still must emphasize his drowsiness to avoid being blamed for foolishness. To spare the feelings of the dog's owner is a thing desirable indeed but not unconditionally. Reason demands that it be considered against a background of more fundamental purposes. If these purposes are not, themselves, terminal, either they will be related to still more fundamental purposes or again blame will be put on the incompleteness of rational consideration, as a result of drowsiness, intoxication, distraction, or any similar factor. Unless the discourse of reason is cut short by some interfering power, the teleological process goes on until it reaches a thing that has unqualifiedly the character of a term, and this thing is what is called the last end.

To remain in the same circle of examples and images, imagine a driver on the winding and dangerous road who coldly runs over a child in order not to expose his own life to any bad chance. He is not drowsy, not intoxicated, and not absent-minded. By saying that he knows very well what he is doing and where he is going, we mean that his consideration of the end is not restricted by any interfering factor and does not fall short of its term. The final end is not involved in the act of a sleepy driver who sees a dog and turns the wheel; neither is it involved in the incompletely rational behavior of the driver who does not turn the wheel until he has realized how sad and angry the dog's owner would be. In both of these cases, something that falls short of complete rationality—call it nature or instinct, or what you will—has taken care of the situation. Such behavior is described as involuntary. An act is not unqualifiedly voluntary unless it proceeds from a judgment which declares, in terminal manner, that it is good to act precisely in this way. Now, to declare in terminal, final, ultimate manner that it is good to do this or to refrain from doing it is precisely to involve the last end.[16]

The difficulties which may be found in this description arise principally from interference by images of concreteness. To say that voluntary action naturally adheres to the last end does not mean that it naturally adheres to the thing which, in truth and reality and wisdom, constitutes the last end. Here, as well as in the case of the closely related notions of good and happiness, the object of necessary and

[16] [See Aquinas, *Summa Theologica,* Ia IIae, q. 6, aa. 1 and 2. Ed.]

natural adherence has the character of a form. Every voluntary action is determinately related to a thing which possesses, for the agent at the time of the action, the character of a final end. Every voluntary action is determinately relative to the final end, although, as experience shows, there is in mankind much disagreement and inconsistency as to the thing in which the character of last end should be placed. For some the last end consists in wealth, for others in power, for others in glory, for others in pleasure, for others in culture, and for others in God. Within the same day of the same man the last end may be placed first in God, then in some created good—say, pleasure—then in another created good—say, honor—and in God again.

In order to understand the meaning of the last end formally understood, it is necessary to refer to some aspects of the general theory of finality. Recall, first, that the opposite and related concepts of means and end admit of combination in all degrees. Let us never think that whatever is a means is thereby entirely denied the character of an end, or that whatever has the character of an end is thereby denied the character of a means. A pure means is a thing that has absolutely no desirability of its own and cannot be desired except as a way leading to a thing desirable. Few things or operations are entirely pure means. On the other hand many things desirable in themselves and for themselves are held desirable in subordination to greater goods. Physical and mental health are not mere means: these are things desirable in their own right; but from this it does not follow that the goods of virtue, in case of conflict, should be sacrificed to good health, and that the physician or the psychiatrist should tell me, with scientific definitiveness, what use I should make of my faculties. The means which is but a means and the end which is but an end are the extremities of a series whose intermediary members combine the character of means and the character of end. Understandably, our mind inclines toward the notions marked by simplicity. A complex and antinomic notion, like that of intermediary end, is constantly threatened by the neighboring notions which are free from antinomy, viz., those of mere means and final end.

Attention should be called, further, to an enlightening relation between the orders of formal and final causality. Let the formal cause be defined as that by reason of which a thing is *what* it is. In relation to the composite, matter is describable as that *out of which* a thing is made; but in relation to the form itself, matter should be described as that *in which* the form resides and that which owes its own determination, its own being such and such, its own whatness, to the form. Clearly, a relation of matter to form obtains, within the order of final causality, between the means and the end. Every means, as such,[17] derives from the end its being what it is, its desirability, its goodness, its intelligi-

[17] This reduplication should be strongly emphasized. The thing which is a means is never exclusively constituted by its being means. Insofar as, independently of its being means, it is a thing, it involves a determination of its own which even may exclude the relation to the end in which there is a question of placing it. In the physical order an example of such a situation would be that of a surgical operation too dangerous to be worth performing. In the moral order, there is the case of placing a morally wrong means at the service of a worthy end. The ethically wrong means does not actually lead to the worthy end considered in its ethical worthiness. It is but seemingly that there is relation of means to end. Some light is shed on this appearance by considering the means in its matter-to-form relation to the end. Not any matter can stand any form; there is necessarily a proportion between form and matter. This proportion is lacking in the case of the morally wrong means believed to be subservient to a morally worthy end. Just as a child would believe that a motor can be made out of wooden parts, so many people who should have an adult conscience believe that the welfare of the civil community can be furthered by perjury, character assassination, etc. Such intrinsically evil actions are matters that cannot bear such a form as the service of the community. All the trouble comes from our failure to realize what this form actually implies.

bility as a thing in the order of final causality. The end is the form of the means; the ulterior end, which is more of an end, is the form of the inferior end, which is more of a means.

There is, within the last end itself, a duality which, in order to be well understood, must be interpreted both in terms of formal causality and in terms of final causality—or, to put it in entirely precise language, in terms of the kind of formal causality which belongs to the end in its relation to the means. Take, for instance, the case of a man who places his last end in what his community calls honor. Respect for the law of God never prevented him from fighting a duel when the code of honor demanded that a duel be fought. Then a day comes when the appeal of pleasure outweighs the power of habitual adherence to honor; this brave man, who so many times risked his life in order to keep his honor clean, lays down honor for the sake of pleasure. It may be a temporary accident and it may be the beginning of hopeless decadence. Clearly, the form of last end, first placed in honor, is now placed in pleasure. But in the order of final causality the end and the end alone has the character of a form. Whatever has the character of a form is end, and whatever has the character of a matter is means. The duality of form and matter discloses, within the last end itself, a duality of means and end. If I place my end in honor I thereby chose honor as supreme means to my last end. That in which the form of last end is placed has, inasmuch as it is bearer of such a form, the character of a means. At this point, it is impossible not to ask the question whether the duality of form and matter in the ultimate end is forever irreducible. The form of last end can be placed in honor, and from honor be transferred to pleasure, and from creature be transferred to God, and from God be transferred, again, to pleasure or honor: such is the uncertainty of our pathways. The natural philosopher is in no position to deny the possibility of a final reduction to unity. But if there exists a situation establishing absolute coincidence between the form of last end and the thing in which this form is placed, this situation is not given in the experience of the natural philosopher.

So far, we have been considering operations of a certain kind, viz., voluntary operations, and their specific character. Only operations fall under our experience; the permanent principle which accounts for the stability of their specific feature can be known only *a posteriori*. We have reached the point where the consideration of the power should supplement that of the operations. The distinctive feature of voluntary acts makes it possible to describe the nature of the will. Only a nominalistic prejudice incompatible with the essence of philosophic analysis would see anything adventurous in the exploration of the power by which man elicits actions characterized by voluntariness. When the prejudice against the powers of the soul does not originate in sheer nominalism, it proceeds from the fear of the accidents which, apparently, have occurred often enough to occasion a stubborn attitude of diffidence. These accidents are: (*a*) the illusion that the powers of the soul are the object of a distinct experience, as if each of us could see by introspection the nature of his understanding or of his will, in the way in which man, according to Descartes, intuitively perceives the thinking nature of his substance; (*b*) the weight of language seems often to have inclined the philosophers to treat the powers of the soul as so many substantial wholes communicating with one another like distinct organs or distinct persons; (*c*) the notion of operative power is philosophic and ontological; this does not mean that it has no part to play in nonphilosophic disciplines; in fact the least philosophically minded of psychologists are not afraid to speak of sight or hearing or memory or imagination. But, like every ontological notion transferred to a field of nonontological science, the notion of power of the soul needs to be reconsidered and reshaped according to the requirements of the new epistemological context. If by mistake such reconsideration has been omitted, there occurs the kind of disorder to which the scientific spirit is most sensitive, for its very principles are at stake.

The preceding descriptions and analyses can be summed up by saying that voluntary operations are essentially relative to an object describable, from slightly different points of view, as the comprehensive good—happiness and the last end. Through the voluntary operations, this relation belongs in essential fashion to the permanent principle by which man elicits the so-called voluntary operations, the will.

At this point the character of formality attributed by the preceding analysis to the object of the will seems to contrast with the concreteness that marks every object of appetition. Let us briefly recall the well-known contrast between knowledge and love with regard to wholeness. Abstraction, as such, is never a hindrance to the perfection of knowledge. It might be misleading to say that knowledge is essentially analytical; in truth, it aims at achieving complete congruence to essential connections. But because the complexes offered by experience contain several essences in contingent relation, the processes of theoretical research always involve some sort and some amount of division. The process of division does hinder the purposes of knowledge when it happens to describe as essential effect of the part what in actuality is essential to the whole or vice versa. Again, the law of theoretical knowledge is one of strict adherence to processes of essential causality, and, so long as the isolation, disassociation, resolution or analysis of object leads to the achievement of such a strict adherence, methods of division unqualifiedly further the perfection of knowledge.

Love and desire, on the contrary, in all their forms and at all levels of perfection, are concerned with wholes. This law follows upon the relation of love's object to existence. Whenever a nonexistent thing is desired, it is desired in relation to existence. What is desired is its coming into existence and ultimately the unique complex made of a thing and its existing in actuality. Any object of desire is a subject of existence and involves all the complexity that its existence requires. Whenever love seems to miss this concern with totality, its genuineness is held dubious.

The formal character attributed to the good, to

happiness, and to the last end seems to conflict with the concreteness of whatever is loved or desired. The expression *bonum in communi,* historically of central importance in the theory of the will, brings forth pictures of isolation and abstraction which would characterize an object of knowledge rather than an object of appetition. That same expression suggests that the particularities of particular goods are left out, and the features common to all good things disengaged from their particular embodiments. At the term of such a process of disassociation, we have an object of knowledge, not an object of love, desire or volition.[18] From slightly different angles, the same could be said of the related concepts of happiness and last end.

In order to remove the difficulty, it suffices to consider the difference between *that which* is loved and *that on account of which* what is loved is loved. That which is loved always has the character of a whole. More exactly, that which is loved necessarily satisfies the requirements of existence with regard to

[18] Even if the question were to bring forth a pure object of knowledge, the abstraction just described would call for serious reservations. Since the good is a transcendent and analogous notion, which contains actually the differences of its inferiors, it does not admit of an abstraction properly so called, but only of an abstraction by confusion.

wholeness. This is where there is a sharp contrast between knowledge and love. As just recalled, the object of knowledge resists certain types of decomposition, but such resistance always evidences the requirements of intelligibility, never those of actual existence. But that on account of which a thing is loved or desired does not need to coincide with the whole of the thing loved or desired. In fact, within the limits of our experience, that on account of which a thing is desired always has the character of an aspect of the thing desired. Let the thing desired be a house. No doubt, the whole house is desired—not a mere aspect of it. But it is on account of some aspect or aspects of the house that the whole of it is desired. If there were a question of pure knowledge, the story might end with the consideration of a single aspect. For instance, I would be interested in a certain house as a work of baroque art, and remain ignorant of whatever aspect of this house is of no relevance for the understanding of baroque art (for example, whether this house is damp). I may on the other hand desire to own a baroque house on account of its being a baroque structure, or by reason of its being a safe shelter, or by reason of its convenient location, or for all these and other reasons. When desire is involved, any *aspect* is a mere "on account of which" or "by reason of which." The object itself comprises, together with the aspect, all the components, known and unknown, of the thing itself. A moneymaker is not suspected of concern for abstractions; yet it can be said that whatever he likes, loves or is interested in, is referred to as "a thing that brings money," and under the form of "the money-bringing."

Even genuine love admits of degrees of genuineness. As is known both to moralists and to metaphysicians, love of friendship is more of a love than love of covetousness, in proportion as the notion of love is more intensely realized in friendship than in covetousness. Consider the disposition of a lover of baroque art who purchases a house not because of its being conveniently located or properly insulated, but exclusively because of its worth as a piece of baroque architecture and decoration. This art lover purchases also convenient location and proper insulation because he is interested in having the baroque thing existentially, and, in existential possession, the aspect of a worthy piece of baroque art cannot be isolated from the other aspects of the thing which is a baroque house. Yet these other aspects may not be intended by the art lover, and, if somebody congratulates him on the nice location and fine insulation of his purchase, he may reply that, not being interested in these qualities of the house, he would be happy to give them to whoever is interested in such location and insulation, if it were possible to separate these advantages from the baroque features.

Such an attitude is appropriate to the kind of love that, according to common ideas, one may feel for a house. But suppose that such an analytical intention concerns a person rather than a thing: it would be interpreted as decisive evidence of ungenuineness, falsehood, and dishonesty. When the object of love is a person, love is expected to be friendship, and if it turns out to be mere covetousness, one thinks that there is falsehood by failure to meet expectation. It is entirely normal to love a lady on account of her kindness and her beauty; but if the lover's intention is so directed as to involve no concern whatsoever for her health, her intelligence, or the perfection of her social manners, the loved object is not treated like another self and love is understood to fall short of friendship. When the notion of love is realized as friendship, in its greater intensity it involves such a demand for totality that the defects of the beloved person are commonly covered by the works of illusion.[19] A lover of ba-

[19] [See Lucretius' description of how the lover views his beloved:

A black love is called "honey-dark," the foul and filthy "unadorned," the green-eyed "Athena's image," the wiry

roque art does not need to develop illusions about the convenient location, fine insulation, etc. of his pur-

---

and wooden "a gazelle," the squat and dwarfish "one of the graces," "all pure delight," the lumpy and ungainly "a wonder," and "full of majesty." She stammers and cannot speak, "she has a lisp"; the dumb is "modest"; the fiery, spiteful gossip is "a burning torch." One becomes a "slender darling," when she can scarce live from decline; another half dead with cough is "frail." Then the fat and full-bosomed is "Ceres' self with Bacchus at breast"; the snub-nosed is "sister to Silenus, or a Satyr"; the thick-lipped is "a living kiss." More of this sort it were tedious for me to try to tell [*Op. cit.*, Bk. IV, lines 1160–1170].

Molière makes much the same point:

. . . Lovers are always observed to extol their choice. Their passion never sees aught to blame in it, and in the beloved all things become lovable. They think their faults perfections, and invent sweet terms to call them by. The pale one vies with the jessamine in fairness; another dark enough to frighten people, becomes an adorable brunette; the lean one has a good shape and is lithe; the stout one has a portly and majestic bearing; the slattern, who has few charms, passes under the name of a careless beauty; the giantess seems a very goddess in their sight; the dwarf is an epitome of all the wonders of Heaven; the proud one has a soul worthy of a diadem; the artful brims with wit; the silly one is very good-natured; the chatterbox is good-tempered; and the silent one modest and reticent. Thus a passionate swain loves even the very faults of those of whom he is enamored [*The Misanthrope,* Act II, Sc. 5, trans. Morris Bishop (New York: Random House, 1957), p. 247].

Ed.]

chase. Or if he does, we suspect that there is affective personification of the thing beloved and that the fellow has a sort of friendship for his baroque house.

The proposition that the object of the will is the comprehensive good means that for the rational appetite any desirable aspect of a thing is desirable on account of its participating in the quality of being good. It is this participation which is expressed, with the decisive simplicity of the great philosophic mysteries, by this part of our initial description: "He thought that it was good to act this way." Let us, again, compare the voluntary act born of the judgment that it is good to act this way, with an act born of, say, an instinctive estimation. To be sure, a nonrational desire is relative to the good, and an object of sense appetition participates in the transcendent good. But, on the level of infrarational life, this participation is not known and an act of sense appetition is not born of the knowledge of the participation of the particular good in the transcendent good. In a very proper sense every action of every agent is related to the last end of all things; yet acting for the sake of an end is the privilege of rational agents inasmuch as the knowledge of the notion of finality pertains only to rational agents. The rational agent alone acts for the sake of an end inasmuch as in him alone action proceeds from the knowledge of a relation to the end. All things, indeed, admit of accomplishment, and many things nonrational are capable of pleasure. But accomplishment and pleasure do not assume the character of happiness unless striving and enjoyment are consciously related to an object understood as congruent to the all-embracing good and consequently capable of satisfying the infinite ambition of a rational nature.

3

Freedom

THE CONSCIOUSNESS OF FREEDOM[1]

LET US ATTEMPT a description of what consciousness tells us on the subject of freedom. We shall avoid as completely as possible the use of terms involving technical elaboration. If it were possible to do without such terms altogether, we would not use any. But this is not possible.

1 [A note shows that in order to show the philosophic presuppositions to which the so-called "argument from the testimony of consciousness" is linked, Professor Simon intended to provide the following as an introduction to

(*a*) The most direct of the data of consciousness concerning freedom is the feeling of a contrast between the free and the non-free event. Our actions exhibit to our inward sense a deeply and vividly different appearance according as they are or are not affected by the modality in virtue of which we call them free. True, there are obscure situations in which we happen to ask "have I acted freely?" and leave the question unanswered. Likewise we are sometimes unable to say with certainty whether a sound has been heard or merely imagined. In order to evaluate the bearing of such doubts, we must realize that in this world of contingency an event A can always be imitated by some event B so that it is not always possible to determine for sure whether an actual experience is that of A or that of B. The existence of an area of confusion and non-typical experiences does not invalidate the meaning of a contrast between typical experiences.

(*b*) The particular modality which characterizes

---

this chapter: (1) a reference to the content of contemporary philosophy for this so-called "argument"; (2) quotations of popular expositions from Thomas Reid, Dugald Stewart, John Stuart Mill (on Sir William Hamilton); (3) evidence for the relation between these popular philosophers and Descartes; (4) some statements on the power of consciousness-intuition. Ed.]

the event that we call free properly resides in choice. It is in the act of doing this rather than that, or of preferring action to abstention, or abstention to action, that we feel free.

(*c*) The obvious components of the feeling of freedom are spontaneity and mastery.

This feeling is violently abolished when our conduct and our destiny are taken in hand by an extraneous force. I slip on the icy ground and mechanical laws get hold of my being without any possibility of resistance: fracture, suffering, a long period of invalidism—this is imposed upon me and I painfully realize my subjection to cosmic nature. But I recover the sense of my freedom as I come to consider this problem of interior life: how shall I receive these pains?—in revolt, or in love?

All this is very clear. But philosophers have given too little attention to experiences which show that an act may appear as both spontaneous and devoid of freedom. I can give or refuse my consent to desires arising from an old passion. So far as consent is concerned I master the situation. I affirm that my consent, or my refusal to consent, is free. As to the desire itself, I cannot annihilate it at will. I realize my subjection to a hated passion as vividly as my subjection to cosmic nature. However, this desire whose presence is imposed upon me with the certainty of anguish proceeds from within myself. It was born of my nature and of my past consents. It is a spontaneous product of my psychological history. Its necessity is "organic, intimate and permanent" and its assertions are "sincere."

In Bergson freedom is described in terms of totality rather than mastery. It is a distinguished kind of spontaneity, viz., the spontaneity of an act proceeding from the depth of the person and consequently from the whole of the person, for the whole of the person is involved in every aspect of the deep self. The energies of the superficial self are external to what is genuine in the self. Bergsonian freedom is freedom from such energies. It is, in a very exacting sense, freedom from coercion—for "coercion" means determination by an external force—but it is not freedom from necessity. This interpretation, first proposed by adversaries of Bergsonism, has been confirmed with decisive authority by an exceptionally intelligent Bergsonist. Vladimir Jankélévitch writes:

The *free* is in one sense the *total* and the *profound.* An act is free in proportion as it constitutes a more truthful and more expressive testimony about my person—not about this oratorical and social part of my person which serves in social relations, but about my necessary and intimate person, the one for which I feel responsible and which is really myself. A free act is a significant set. In a determinate act on the contrary what is most partial and most insignificant in my person finds a refuge. It is a superficial and local act. Freedom so conceived would not be anything else than a kind of necessity—this is what all great metaphysicians have understood—but it is an organic, intimate, and permanent necessity. Considered as a requirement, freedom implies for us the duty to remain, as best we can, contemporary to our own actions and never to fly into the past of efficient causes or the future of rationalizations. It is the enemy of fiction. It is opposed by hypocritical pleas and abstract rhetoric. And then its name is sincerity.[2]

Inasmuch as Bergsonian freedom remains a kind of necessity, it may be considered that its notion lacks an essential feature, viz., the power by which the will overcomes necessity. On the other hand, inasmuch as it requires the commitment of the whole self, it seems to involve a feature foreign to the concept of freedom. Among the experiences in which freedom reveals itself in the most convincing way, one must cite some cases in which the deep self is itself divided. Thus, in the example described above [p. 77], it would be very arbitrary to contend that any of the conflicting forces belongs to the superficial self.

[2] Vladimir Jankélévitch, *Bergson* (Paris: Alcan, 1931), p. 103.

(*d*) Finally, the acts described as free are characterized by the moral reactions which accompany them: feelings of lawfulness, of merit and demerit, of responsibility, etc.

And thus we have already passed beyond the limit of what the experience of consciousness teaches us about freedom antecedently to the analysis of freedom's causes. In spite of our set purpose to limit ourselves to the immediate data of experience, we could not fail to use, in this brief description, interpretative instruments involving a large amount of theoretical elaboration—e.g., the concepts of choice, of spontaneity and of mastery. In our endeavor to reach the absolutely empirical background of our experience, we stopped half way. It was impossible to go further without giving up speech and thought. But from the spot actually reached in this process of abstraction in reverse toward the primitive experimental background, it is easy to locate the goal that we cannot attain. Without going further, we can see further, to the end of the road. Indeed, the more we strip our experience of the interpretative concepts born of rational reflection, the more the testimony of consciousness becomes simple and confused. If it were possible to withhold completely the operation of philosophical reason, the pure experience that we would reach would be reduced to a firm but extremely confused assertion of the existence of our freedom.

Contrary to the postulations of some spiritualistic philosophies, the intuition of consciousness does not disclose, without further ado, the nature of our acts, of our powers, and of our substance. Consciousness tells me that I think, that I will, that I freely choose, and that I am. But in order to know what thought is, what the will is, what freedom is; in order to know whether I am a substance or a bundle of phenomena, a piece of extension or a spirit, or a composite of body and spirit, awareness of my activities does not suffice. It is necessary to subject these activities to analysis, to disengage their forms from surrounding contingencies, to compare, to judge and to reason; in a word, to exercise science and philosophy.[3] No intuition can be substituted

[3] The act of intelligence in man is not primarily an act of consciousness: it is primarily an act of knowing the world. Direct and primary intellection has for its object physical nature, not the spiritual self. The views of Saint Thomas on the secondary and reflexive character of intellectual consciousness are opposed to: (*a*) the idealistic theory of thought having as its primary object its own accidents, its ideas or concepts taken in the sense of mental realities. Saint Thomas discards such interpretations in well-known passages (*De Anima,* III, lect. 8; *Summa Theologica,* I, q. 85, a. 2) in which he declares that the intelligible species is not *that which* is known (*id quod*

for the work of the reason and dispense with its difficulties: this holds for the soul as well as for

---

intelligitur), but *that by means of which* the object known is known (*id quo intelligitur*), except in the reflective process in which the idea is taken as the object and where that which was *quo* becomes *quod*; (*b*) the spiritualistic theory according to which the human intellect would be primarily turned inward and would have as its first object, not physical reality, but the human spirit itself.

In Cartesianism, spiritualism and idealism are allied and perhaps identified. Most modern theories of consciousness bear the mark of this alliance or identification. In the pre-Cartesian era, the Socratic and Augustinian formulas of consciousness had often been interpreted in the sense of a realistic spiritualism. In fact, as a good realist one can admit that the idea is pure *quo* and affirm that the first *quod* attained by the human intellect is the human spirit. Let us note, however, that any theory which declares that the knowledge of self is prior to the knowledge of physical nature implies difficulties which make idealism hard to avoid in the framework of the modern problematic.

As concerns the *bearing* of the experience of consciousness, Saint Thomas makes a contrast between knowledge of the individual soul—of my soul—and knowledge of the human soul considered in its universal nature. Because my reflection attests to my acts and through them to my powers and to the substance of my soul, it suffices that my soul be *presented* to my intellect. If, on the contrary, it is a question of knowing the human soul in its universal nature, the presence of my soul does not resolve anything: what is needed is a far more difficult search and one that

nature. It is up to the spontaneous philosophy of common sense, and later to the technically worked-out philosophy of the philosophers to render explicit and distinct what immediate experience presents in confusion.

At this point, some elaboration on common sense is needed. If common sense enjoyed the essential unity of a power or function, it should be said that it did a great deal, in the scientific and philosophic domains, to deserve its bad reputation. But what the expression "common sense" designates does not

---

runs serious risks of error. (Cf. *Summa Theologica,* I, q. 87, a. 1.)

This knowledge of the individual soul, insured by the very presence of the soul to the intellect, is indeed what we call the experience of consciousness. To characterize the sort of information which it procures, Saint Thomas declares that it answers questions of the type *whether it is,* and that questions of the type *what is it* belong to the inquiry concerning the universal nature of the soul. (Cf. *De Veritate,* q. 10, a. 8.)

To understand the problem clearly, we must refer to the passage in the *Posterior Analytics* (Bk. II, Ch. 1), in which Aristotle discusses *scientific questions,* and to the commentary of Saint Thomas on the same passage. Compare also the lucid exposition of Maritain on the meaning of these questions in *The Degrees of Knowledge,* Appendix III—"What God Is" (New York: Scribner's, 1959).

For the application of the principles dealing with the knowledge of the soul by itself to the case of the will, see *Summa Theologica,* I, q. 87, a. 4.

enjoy any functional unity. It is an aggregate of propositions, none of which requires, in the mind that assents to it, the refinements of a special and technical training. Not all these propositions are known to all men, and it is absurd to claim that they are equally clear to all. But it is true that no man ever needed to go to school in order to be ready to assent, at least in implicit fashion, to a common-sense proposition. A more specific formula would imply arbitrary exclusions.

In rough outline it can be said that common sense comprises three kinds of propositions: propositions of philosophic character which are the starting point of every philosophy and every science; propositions dictated by the leanings of the imagination, and propositions expressing a practical vision of the physical world. Science normally conflicts with the imagery of common sense according to which the earth is flat, people at the antipodes have their heads hanging downwards, light bodies cannot fall as fast as heavy ones, the quotient $\frac{1}{2\pi}$ does not remain constant as the radius of the circle increases, substance is something dense and hard like a desk made of oak, etc. It is only by accident that the images of common sense agree with the expressions of the scientific or philosophic mind. As to the practical vision of the world proposed by common sense, it sometimes conflicts with science: thus, for physics the earth and the feather attract each other, whereas for common sense the earth attracts the feather, though weakly, and the feather does not attract the earth at all. Sometimes science takes over the common-sense vision of the world: thus, the concept of chance occurrence as an unpredictable event is a common-sense notion accepted and modified by science. With respect to common sense as philosophy, it happens to offer to science a resistance which is limited, reducible and more apparent than real.[4]

It is most important never to confuse the rudimentary philosophy professed by common sense

[4] This happens or may happen when science substitutes, for the ontological concept which common sense has of a certain thing, a concept formed according to the laws belonging to positive thought, which is nonontological or anti-ontological. The two concepts, expressed by the same word, can become the subjects of propositions contradictory in character: thus, for common sense simultaneity is absolute, but for physics it is not. To speak correctly, the opposition has to do with the laws of the formation of concepts: on account of the different laws which governed their formation, the concepts refer to objects which are different in some respect and, therefore, can enter into propositions which are true in spite of the apparent contradiction.

with the practical vision or the imagery which are the other components of common sense. It is also very important to realize that common sense as a philosophy is nothing else than philosophic reason itself, in the state of imperfect operation within which it remains confined until technical instruments have been provided by the labor of schools. Lastly, it is necessary to distinguish, within common sense as philosophy, several sorts of propositions, several types of cognitions.

(*a*) First, the axioms of the universal reason: the principles of identity, of noncontradiction, of the excluded middle; the principle of rationality; the principles of efficient causality, of material causality, and of final causality. Perfect accuracy would demand that these axioms be described as antecedent to all philosophy and placed above all philosophy, that of common sense included.

(*b*) Common sense contains the statement of philosophic facts distinguished by their formal significance. The typology of objects, which is one with the typology of concepts, determines the typology of facts; the intelligible distribution of objects, within any system of interpretation, determines the intelligible distribution of facts, their rank, their hierarchical position and their significance. Although the whole system of the statements of facts belongs to the material part of thought—for the formal part belongs to the principles—some facts are more material, and some are more formal in character. "Something exists"; "there exist, in the world of our experience, things diverse by species"; "all things perceptible to the senses are subject to motion": these common-sense facts are the most formal among the philosophic facts.

(*c*) Over and above axiomatic propositions, provided with immediate and rational evidence, and statements of facts, provided with immediate and experimental evidence, common sense comprises demonstrated propositions which constitute, on the level of common sense, a philosophy properly so called. Axioms are the principles of science rather than science itself, and facts are but the material of science: this holds for philosophic disciplines as well as for the other sciences. We shall consider two examples of such common-sense demonstrations. One is relative to God and the other to freedom.

There was once a time when literature celebrated the power of unsophisticated intellects able to perceive, naturally and simply, evidences of the divine existence in the infinity of a starry sky or in the mystery of a child's eyes. Today such considerations would be badly outmoded. Literary gentlemen have become conscious of the virtues of sophistication, and do not allow themselves to be outdone by the sarcastic negations of atheistic positivists and amateur metaphysicians. Genuine metaphysicians alone refrain from mockery: for they recognize, in totally unsophisticated reasonings, the essence of scientific reasonings. The demonstrations of philosophers assume, in common sense, a *state* which sometimes makes them hard to recognize. It is important to understand what this state actually consists of.

An old sailor used to say that at sea, far away from any land, man knows that he is a very small thing, and thinks of God. A beginner metaphysician would not fail to remark that the vastness of the ocean, being altogether quantitative and material, and the small size of the human body, in the same quantitative and material order, are of no metaphysical relevance. He would not fail, further, to reply to Pascal that nothing is learned about human nature by remarking that man is bigger than a mite and smaller than a nebula. But Pascal also wrote the page of the thinking reed, where a metaphysical vision is expressed with lucid accuracy. The quantitative images of the mite and the nebula can be used as symbolic of ontological concepts and thus contribute to manifest the greatness and the misery of man. By assuming the character of a symbol, an image puts itself at the service of thought and no longer imposes its own conveniences upon thought, as it did in the antecedently described situation. In the fragment of the mite, metaphysics remains engaged in its imaginative concomitants: this does not mean that it is false or ineffective. Inside a system of images, thought can be entirely sound and true. The dangers involved in such a state are felt mostly when the system of the primitive images loses its coherence. This generally happens when a man of common sense experiences the intoxication of half science. Then astronomy becomes a redoubtable adversary of metaphysics: thought is bewildered by an overwhelming experience of broken images. ("Son of man, you cannot say, or guess, for you know only a heap of broken images . . ."—T. S. Eliot.[5]) In the old sailor the metaphysics of common sense, untroubled by scholasticism, expressed itself with complete safety. The image of my smallness in front of the universe symbolizes the *insufficiency* of the things of this world, which insufficiency is revealed to me by the feeling of my helplessness.

In the anxiety of the seaman the whole world discloses its nothingness and its inability to exist, save by the virtue of the One Who Is. The logical

[5] *The Waste Land,* lines 20–22, in *Collected Poems of T. S. Eliot,* 1909–1962 (New York: Harcourt, Brace & World, 1963, and London: Faber & Faber).

structure of the proof is complete. Here, as well as in the greatest metaphysicians, it all boils down to the experience of a reality so unachieved that it would be foreclosed from existence if it were not given existence by a Being whose plenitude both corresponds to whatever plenitude is found in this reality and contrasts with its unachievement. The experience of change leads to the motionless source of all change, the experience of causal dependences to the first and independent cause, that of contingency leads to the necessary being, that of participated perfections to subsistent perfection, and the existence of finality leads to the intellect which is its own action and its own end. All that is known to the old sailor. But for lack of technical elaboration, the metaphysical thoughts of common sense are living and active only within an atmosphere saturated with images; above this atmosphere they are like the dove of Kant, and exhaust themselves in a vacuum.[6] They are not communicable in the

[6] "The light dove, cleaving the air in her free flight, and feeling its resistance, might imagine that its flight would be easier in empty space. It was thus that Plato left the world of the senses, as setting too narrow limits to the understanding, and ventured out beyond it on the wings of the ideas, in the empty space of the pure understanding" (*Critique of Pure Reason,* translation by Norman Kemp Smith [New York: St. Martin's, 1965], p. 47).

same way as disengaged concepts. Their way of being communicated resembles their way of living: they are communicated together with the imaginative wholes within which they live. When the images retain, in the transition from one mind to another, their native energy, the metaphysical thoughts existing within them are communicated with a vivaciousness that the abstract conversations of scholars often lack.

In the case of freedom, in order to understand that a demonstration substantially identical with that of the philosophers belongs to common sense, it suffices to remark that many persons, without having gone to schools of philosophy or any school, consider it obvious that a man cannot be held responsible for acts committed in sleep, early childhood, delirium, insanity, and more generally in a state in which the reason is not in actual use. The argument which bears out this conviction can be summed up as follows: the actual exercise of the reason is a necessary condition of the actual possession of freedom. Moreover, between reason and freedom there is an intelligible relation: one recognizes in the reason the explanatory principle or essential cause of freedom. Thus between the subject "man" and the predicate "endowed with freedom," the connection is established, according to common sense, by the mediation of the quality of rational being, and the middle term supplied by rationality is attributed a worth greater than that of a merely factual bond: it is *because* of rationality that the predicate "endowed with freedom" belongs to the subject "man." This argumentation bears all the characteristics of an *a priori* and explanatory demonstration. So far as logical essences are concerned, the philosophers do not do any better and do not do anything else. But it is their job to render the demonstration more intelligible, more powerful, more certain and more rigorous, more fruitful and more enlightening, and more certainly communicable, through processes of clarification. (One of the main purposes of such clarification is to protect the logical essence of demonstration against the accidents which can take place at any time in the system of the concomitant images. But philosophers often happen to do their job poorly. Instead of removing the false notion of freedom suggested by an imaginative representation of the free act, a philosophy of freedom may happen to be merely a more or less consistent rationalization of images of disorder.)

We must bear all this in mind in interpreting the experience of freedom. Sheer experience would procure no more than an extremely confused assertion of existence. In order to go beyond such empirical confusion, it is necessary to philosophize, and this is what common sense hastens to do, without waiting for a technically elaborated philosophy. It is now easy to account for the accidents that the consciousness of freedom suffers both in common sense and in the philosophers. The common-sense man interprets his experience with the help of rudimentary concepts and of principles which, though not formally expressed, are strongly felt. The requirements of social life, which so often act as a disturbing factor, may well play here the part of effective stimulation as well as that of helpful safeguard—for the development of a sense of responsibility, by strengthening the ethical feelings which accompany the free act and contribute to distinguish it from an act that is not free, renders the experience of freedom more vivacious and more perceptive. When the man of common sense reaches mature judgment, belief in freedom results in him from the nonsystematic but vital cooperation of an experience of consciousness and a process of rational interpretation. In order to express itself in appropriate concepts and language, this rational interpretation lacks only the technical refinements of a philosophy cultivated into a virtue of the intellect.

Again, the participation of men in the philosophic

capacity of common sense is unequal. The philosophy of common sense is a set of truths which can be obtained without any technically elaborated apparatus and which are actually possessed, in varying degree of clarity and intensity, by every normal mind. But in order that the mind should actually possess cognitions normally accessible to it, many conditions are required and it is not certain —at least, it is not obvious—that all these conditions are realized in most cases. Besides the unqualifiedly pathological cases, in which the working of the reason is impaired by organic or psychological disturbances, a man whose mind has not been regularly trained toward truth by an appropriate education—a man in whom moral debasement affects the lucidity of understanding; most of all, a man born in a social environment saturated with error—fails to satisfy the conditions required for the full possession of common sense. Philosophers are not the only ones to whom it happens that common sense is lost. It is impossible to rule out *a priori* the possibility of a society in which the sense of freedom would be weakened or impaired in most persons. A fatalistic religion, the belief in the universal influence of magical causality, or the habit of servitude may well bring about such a situation.

In philosophers the belief in freedom of choice is exposed to particularly serious dangers. At the beginning of his inquiry the philosopher finds in his consciousness the assertion of freedom. But instead of letting life, as other men do, teach him gradually, without haste and without drama, unconsciously or almost unconsciously, a concept of freedom destined never to be confronted by the difficulties and the risks of an explicit formulation, he is soon challenged to answer the question *what is freedom?* A philosopher cannot afford to be satisfied with statements of existence. He is supposed to know not confusedly but distinctly what he is talking about when he says, for instance, that free acts exist. It often happens that the mind of the philosopher is, all at once, caught by a system which *a priori* makes freedom impossible. Let us not expect the testimony of consciousness to hold in check the power of *a priori*. Experience fights an unequal fight when it comes into conflicts with the hard requirements of the metaphysical, aesthetic, and moral vision of the universal order. If it is possible to change the conviction of a man who denies freedom of choice on the ground of a philosophical *a priori*, it is by destroying this *a priori*, not by stressing the persuasive power of experience. Philosophy, whenever it disagrees with experience, has no trouble to show that what is called experience is really but an illusion. Assuming that the philosopher is so happy as to escape the systematic forms of error, working out the concept of freedom remains a difficult enterprise in which occasions to err are innumerable. What happens if the inquiry issues in a poorly constructed concept? Either the philosopher keeps asserting the existence of freedom (but what he is talking of is not true freedom), or he rejects the concept of freedom as a logical monster, a product of imagination, devoid of real meaning. As an apprentice philosopher, I hold from my inner experience the certitude of my freedom. But soon I am taught that the concept of free act involves the beginning without a cause, that of determination without a determining form, that of uncreated activity in a creature, that of absolute spontaneity, etc. By declaring that free choice does not exist, I get rid as best I can of unbearable absurdities. The violence done to experience is here the inevitable result of failure in conceptual analysis.

The fact that a great number of philosophers deny the reality of freedom can be easily explained without casting any doubt on the certitude of consciousness data. The experience of free choice is certain, but it is extremely confused. By reason of this confusion it seems that the testimony of consciousness cannot constitute a distinct argument for freedom; rather, the testimony of consciousness is the experimental point of departure of the rational inquiry designed to show all at once what free choice is and how and why and under what conditions it necessarily proceeds from the nature of the reason and from the nature of the will.

FREEDOM OF CHOICE AS FREEDOM OF JUDGMENT

Such is the contrast between cognition and appetition, that we often fail to see how intimately the will remains united, in all its activities, with the acts of the understanding. It is misleadingly convenient to imagine the understanding and the will after the fashion of two biological individuals. Treating distinct powers of the same agent as if they were separate substances is a naïve blunder which commonly renders the so-called "faculty psychology" suspect to minds possessed of a keen sense for the features of active unity and interpenetration of the parts by one another which characterize living things and particularly things endowed with a psychological life. According to the construct of imagination, the will, once it is brought into existence, would elicit its operation autonomously, like an adult individual which no longer depends upon its generator. Considering that every act of the will proceeds from a judgment which expresses the desirability of a thing, it is all-important to realize that the dependence of the will upon the practical judgment holds not only in the order of finality but also in that of formal causality.

Clearly, the judgment which declares that a thing is desirable plays an essential role in the order of final causality. The practical judgment causes the act of the will not only by proposing an end for it but also by constituting its form. The practical judgment is the formal cause of the appetition that follows upon it. The final cause is an extensive cause, but the formal cause is intensive. The act of the will owes to the practical judgment the entirety of its specific being—of its being such and such, of its structure, of its way of existing—just as a machine owes to the nature and arrangement of its parts the entirety of its determination as such and such a machine. Accordingly, necessity and liberty, which are formal modes of the act of willing, are primarily modes of judgment. They belong to judgment before they belong to the will. There is no freedom of the will without freedom of judgment. There is no freedom in the appetite if the form from which the appetition proceeds is uniquely determined.

Liberum arbitrium is free judgment. Unless judgment is free, the will exercises its operations in a uniquely determined way, as fire burns and the liver secretes bile. The problem is to designate the conditions under which a judgment escapes the necessity of unique determination.

From the standpoint defined by the purpose of this inquiry we may represent the activities of the intellect as a multiplicity set in order by a polar opposition. Judgments relative to essential, intelligible, evident, and necessary truths make up one of the poles. Here, demonstrated propositions—i.e., propositions brought to a state of evidence through the labor of the mind—center on immediately evident premises. Here, the highest function of the mind, i.e., the ability to perceive the necessity of the first principles, gathers around itself what is best, most finished, and most scientific in the sciences. Here, an absolute necessity obtains not only on the part of the object but also on the part of the judgment; for the mind, when confronted with an obvious proposition, elicits its assent with the spontaneity and the inflexible necessity of a natural process. Here, everything would be luminous and actual if it were not that our intelligence is bound, in all its phases and domains, by a law of gradual accomplishment and never-ending progress.

Let this extremity of our intellectual structure be called *the pole of rational determination.*

Propositions capable of determining the assent of the mind with unqualified necessity are but a small part of the material that our mind has to deal with. Scientific disciplines, as they are understood in academic courses and treatises, comprise only a small nucleus of certainties hard enough to remove all wavering and all contingency from assent. In its effort to achieve science, the human mind has actually constructed systems comprising a broad and changing set of beliefs and opinions more or less successfully ordered by axiomatic premises and fully demonstrated conclusions. Some propositions are held as no more than probable, some are treated as altogether provisional tools of research, and many propositions are guaranteed only by the good faith of a colleague whose experiments and computations have not been repeated by anyone. Thus, some sections of scientific disciplines are placed at a great distance from the pole of rational determination. Yet they constantly undergo its attraction; if they did not, they would soon drop out of the synthesis animated by the principles and achievements of science.

But when there is a question of human action, choice plays an essentially different role in the causation of assent. In scientific disciplines the countless circumstances which make it necessary to deliberate, and to work out opinions on the basis of unsatisfactory data, are defective and uncongenial to the spirit of theoretical truth. On the contrary, a man of action sees nothing abnormal in the choices that action ceaselessly demands of him. He hates incertitude, ambiguous information, incomplete files, answers which wander away from the questions, decisions made on insufficient data, careless collaborators, and late trains: all these are defective circumstances which prevent the principles of action from asserting themselves and give the will no chance to exercise its mastery, for they do not leave it much of a choice.

To understand the true character of action and practical intelligence, one must consider the felicitous and by no means exceptional circumstances in which we are aware of possessing all the data required for a wise decision. Let it be supposed, further, that the instruments of our action are so dependable that there is no danger of missing our end. Our decision retains the character of a choice; no objective obviousness imposes itself upon our mind with the unique determination of an axiomatic premise or a demonstrated conclusion. At the upper limit of this judicative system, all admixture of hesitancy has disappeared; choice is made in full light and attains the climax of its intelligibility. Hesitancy is contrary to the dynamism of choice, for what makes us hesitate is the fear of erring, of missing our goal, of choosing an illusory means—in one word, of having only the appearance of a choice. Thus there exists in our mind, independently of all ignorances and absurdities, a principle whose proper effect is the indifference of judgment. A *pole of practical indifference* is set in opposition to the pole of rational determination. Again, in scientific matters, the inability of the object to cause a uniquely determined judgment always results from some insufficiency on the part of the mind: such is not the case at the pole of practical indifference and in the area in which its attraction obtains. Here, it is a positive reality, not a privation or limitation which causes the indifference of the judgment. It is a force, not a lack of force, and this force is a thing normal and good—witness the feelings of joy, of expansion, of orderly and fruitful life by which its operation is accompanied when there is no interference by any factor of perplexity.

The force which holds in check the determining power of the practical object has been described in Chapter 2 of this book: it is the spontaneous, natural, necessary, and nonvoluntary adherence of the will to the comprehensive good; it is the natural desire for happiness; it is the necessary volition of the last end. By reason of its being a living relation to the comprehensive good, the will invalidates the claim of any particular good to bring about a determinate judgment of desirability. At the instant when the attraction of a thing good in some respect inclines the mind to utter the proposition "this is good for me," the infinite ambition of the will reverses the perspective. The thing which is good only in a certain respect discloses uncongenial aspects, and the proposition "this is not good for me" fights with its contradictory for the assent of the mind.

A simple comparison may help to understand how the necessary appetition of the good causes indifferent judgment in relation to particular goods. Let us imagine persons traveling, in a night without moon and without stars, toward a house in the midst of a forest. One window is lighted but as soon as the travelers have seen it, a capricious pathway makes them lose sight of it. They are near their goal but are not coming closer to it. The lighted window guides them for a short while—then disappears, reappears, and disappears again. The travelers understand that the path turns around the house. When they are on one of the three dark sides there is nothing to direct them. If they want to arrive before daybreak, they will walk straight toward the light, through bushes and ditches, as soon as they perceive it again.

A particular good is to the power of willing what a partially lighted thing is to the power of seeing. The particular good is able to act upon the will by bringing about the proposition "this is good for me." This proposition would be definitively assented to, and the act of the will would follow with necessity if, of all aspects of the particular good, only the desirable one were perceived. Likewise the travelers would not wander away from their goal if they remained on the lighted side of the house. But just as three sides of the house fail to act upon sight, so some aspects of the particular good fail to attract the will. At this point the analogy proves deficient: the non-lighted aspect of a partially lighted thing does not bring about any act in the power of seeing, but the non-desirable aspect of the partially desirable thing is of such nature as to cause a negative act, a movement of aversion whose form is the proposition "this is not good for me." Whether the desirable and the detestable nearly balance each other or whether one of the two greatly outweighs the other is but of accidental significance. The least element of goodness suffices to cause the affirmative practical proposition and the movement of attraction; the least element of non-goodness suffices to cause the negative practical proposition and the movement of aversion. The mixed character of the particular good guarantees the indifference of the judgment—provided however that the mind turns around the partially good thing and considers both its goodness and its non-goodness.

The center of the problem is now at hand. We have to determine how and under what conditions the necessary adherence of the will to the comprehensive good entails the indifference of the practical judgment. The travelers, having understood that they are indefinitely turning around their goal and, everytime they see it, soon lose sight of it again, think of the legends in which a bewitched horse takes his rider through unknown lands and long spaces of time. Everything happens as if a magic force constrained them to turn in a circle instead of advancing. Inasmuch as the will is dedicated to the good, i.e., to a good free from qualifications and desirable in all respects, the very presence of the will in act reveals an infinite distance between particular goods and the comprehensive good. The proposition "this is good for me," loses its impetus against the unlimited demands of the rational nature. A practical proposition, if it is affirmative, cannot be true in an absolute sense unless it regards the very object of the will. Accordingly the negative practical proposition has already appeared. Under the determining impulse of the will, itself determined by its natural object, the intellect has turned about the partially desirable and partially detestable thing. Neither the desirable nor the detestable is strong enough to impose itself upon the mind. Both are limited. The practical intellect considers the goodness of things in relation to the requirements of the will, which requirements admit of no limit. The will is naturally too determined; it is naturally determined by too great and too strong an object for any particular goodness to coincide determinately with its desire. *The indifference of the practical judgment does not originate in any indetermination of intellect or will, it originates in the natural superdetermination of the rational appetite.*

But what conditions must be satisfied for this cause of indifference to operate actually? In order to answer this question we propose to examine some typical examples of causal relations, beginning with the cases in which determinism is most obvious.

1. An event of nature such as the action of an acid upon organic matter is, by general agreement, a

perfectly determinate thing. If someone claims that he can place his hand in concentrated sulphuric acid without suffering any damage, and performs a demonstration before witnesses, we shall make the following hypotheses: (*a*) in spite of appearance, the liquid is not concentrated sulphuric acid; (*b*) the demonstrator has not actually placed his hand in the acid, but his skin was covered with a protective substance. If neither of these hypotheses stands the examination of the facts, we shall try other hypotheses of the same kind. We may have to confess that we do not know what actually happened. We may even go so far as to consider the possibility of a supernatural intervention. But we shall never accept the theory of an acid's indifference to cause or not to cause the destruction of a definite matter. Such a theory is too absurd. There are many things that we do not know, but we are absolutely sure that a chemical reaction, when all its conditions are realized, takes place necessarily. Its form is the very nature of the chemicals involved, its mover is their natural tendency to act and react according to their nature; this tendency is really identical with their nature. If a reaction did not take place when all its conditions are satisfied, things would not be as they are. They would both be and not be. If some primitives attribute to natural energies a character of caprice and indifference, it is either because they conceive them after the patterns of free wills or because they postulate frequent preternatural interventions capable of invisibly suppressing a condition required for the production of an event.

2. If an event of nature depends upon a complex system of conditions, as is the case with the development of an organism, determinism is less obvious but we know that it is no less real. In order that this maple seed, which just fell on the ground, should become an adult plant, it must escape innumerable factors of destruction; it is necessary, further, that all the surrounding natures should give it positive cooperation by supplying food, an appropriate amount of heat and light, etc. We shall refrain from unconditional prediction because we have no way to make sure that all necessary conditions are and will be realized.

But we shall not hesitate to utter a conditional prediction: if all the conditions required for the development of the seed and the young plant are realized, this seed will one day become an adult plant, according to its species. To question it we would have, as in the simpler case of a laboratory reaction, to imagine that things both are and are not what they are.

3. With regard to operations regulated by cognitions, anthropomorphic imagination, which is famous for the tricks it plays on the primitives, plays also very ugly tricks on civilized people. It obstinately suggests that the bird which jumps from branch to branch, in entirely unpredictable fashion, masters its movements and inclinations. The best way to overcome anthropomorphism in these matters is to know ourselves better and to understand how things happen in the nonrational part of our activity.

Let us consider in the first place reflex actions. Some of them—e.g., the contractions of the digestive tract—are purely biological processes where cognition does not play any role. Others depend formally on sensations. As an example of the second genus consider the graphic reflex described by Georges Dwelshauvers.[7] The subject is directed to hold a pencil motionless on the surface of a recorder. He watches a swinging pendulum or listens to the beating of a metronome, or closes his eyes and imagines an oscillating object. The curve records the movements—conscious in some, unconscious in others, but described by all as entirely involuntary, which mark the rhythm of the pendu-

[7] *Traité de psychologie*, second edition (Paris: Payot, 1934), pp. 274–275.

lum, the metronome, or the imagined oscillating object.

It is hard to define philosophically the way in which the perception or the image causes movement in this case. But it is beyond doubt that between the perception or the image and the movement there is strict correspondence, and that cognition plays, in regard to movement, the part of a uniquely determined form, which admits of no contrary.

4. The movements resulting from habit take place in proximity to reflex action. I enter an apartment building which I recently left after having lived in it for a long time. Here is the mail box which used to be mine: I examine it as if it could still contain my mail. Letters addressed to an unknown person make me understand that my action was absurd. The movement was elicited because the idea of not eliciting it came too late. Until I read the unknown name, the imperative representation of the habitual movement was in control of my imagination, and my reason was busy elsewhere. As there was no conflict, the representation has stimulated in a determined and determining way the motor tendency born of habit.

5. In order to find an example of an instinctive judgment not seriously modified by rational activity let us turn to the broad area of the infelicitous

reaction of instinct. It often happens that the line of behavior suggested by instinct is disapproved by reason as soon as rational control is restored. A fire suddenly breaks out in a theatre: several persons are killed in a panic. By the next day it is well established that there would have been no casualties if the audience had not been panic-stricken; if everyone had remained cool-headed and had understood that slow motion was much less dangerous than a rush toward a narrow exit. But no one remained cool-headed, which is the same as to say that the working of reason was suspended in everyone. At the sight of the flames, the instinct of self-preservation alone acted, and the speech uttered by this instinct, "You must run away quickly," was not held in check by any opposite speech. The determinate judgment gave birth to an equally determinate desire and an equally determinate act.

6. By "animal intelligence" we generally designate the principle of nonrational estimations which bear the mark of individual experience and which are ceaselessly transformed by the acquisitions of experience. Whereas the behavior of insects is mostly instinctive, that of the higher vertebrates is remarkably capable of adjustment to the circumstances. If the question of animal intelligence in man is so poorly known, it is probably because it is

very difficult to separate, even incompletely, the processes pertaining to animal intelligence from the rational processes which penetrate them intimately. Yet the cases in which the judgment of animal intelligence conflicts with that of reason clearly disclose the nonrational essence of our animal intelligence.

Two men are about to undergo the same minor operation. Both are aware that the dangers involved are hardly greater than those present in the circumstances of daily life. One of the men considers that whoever drives a car and works in a factory should be able to undergo this minor operation without being particularly moved. He no longer thinks about it. In him the nonrational sense of safety and danger works in harmony with the reason.

The other man makes the same reasoning and waits for the day of the operation with increasing anxiety. True, his reason tells him that he is not more likely to die that day than the day he has his horseback ride, but the nonrational sense of safety and danger—one of the functions of animal intelligence—fills his mind with terrifying visions: a distraction of the anesthetist may cause death by asphyxiation; a loose thread may result in a fatal hemorrhage; an accident in aseptic precautions may entail a fatal infection. If the control of the reason weakens, the nonrational judgment of danger fills the soul with a fear which will not disappear until all danger is removed. It may even outlast the period of danger.

7. Thus, nonrational processes, whether they be physical or psychic, relatively simple or particularly complex, never admit, on the part of their *active form*, of the indifference which makes the act of choosing possible. A judgment of animal intelligence affects the appetite in a uniquely determined way, just as a chemical reaction is caused, with unique determination, by the nature of the chemicals involved. Differences are very great if we consider the observable regularity of events, the possibility of prediction and control, the part of contingency and chance, but they are null if one considers the only thing relevant for the theory of freedom—viz., the relation existing between the appetite and the formal cause of its action.

When this formal cause is a judgment of reason it sometimes is determinate and sometimes indifferent. In the first case the act of will is merely natural; in the second case it is free.

Clearly, there is no indifference in the judgment by which the intellect presents to the will, as absolutely desirable, the comprehensive good. Many particular practical judgments are also devoid of indifference. In the course of a scientific reading my attention is attracted by a beautiful theory: I like the truth that it sketches. I am anxious to know it. This love and this desire are experienced in the way proper to passions, although they are acts of the will. I have the power to suspend the exercise of these acts, but I cannot substitute contrary acts for them. I could have stopped my reading at the preceding page, but having actually pursued it until the theory was outlined, my intellect has recognized its good in the foreshadowed truth and has uttered a determinate judgment of desirability. Suppose that I persist in my design to know this theory. As I consider its difficulties, I go through phases of discouragement; but the remembrance of past difficulties which were overcome, indeed, stirs in me feelings of hope. It is in my power to yield to discouragement or to make hope prevail in my soul, but it is not in my power to undergo or not to undergo a phase of discouragement when the difficulty appears. It is not in my power to undergo or not to undergo a movement of hope when the remembrance of past difficulties gives me a reason to hope. The judgment which brings forth the difficulty of the enterprise and the judgment which brings forth my chances to succeed appear determinately in my mind according as the course of my thoughts brings to the foreground the difficulty to be overcome or the energies which make it possible for me to overcome it. I shall also go through phases of audacity when I consider how beautiful it is to solve a difficulty, and phases of fear as I consider the possibility of failure. In case of final failure it will not be in my power to experience or not to experience a feeling of sadness and irritation. In case of final success, it will not be in my power to experience or not to experience a feeling of joy. Just as the judgments of sense, instinct and animal intelligence, which are always determinate and never indifferent, bring about in the animal appetite nonfree movements that are called passions or emotions, so the judgments of reason bring about in the will sentiments which are natural acts, not free acts, so long as the conditions of the indifferent judgment are not realized.

It is commonly said that deliberation is a necessary condition of indifference in practical judgment and of freedom in choice. This proposition certainly holds in the most frequent cases, which are also the clearest, and the most significant in terms of human interest. What the indifference of practical judgment requires as its proper condition is the perception of the discrepancy between the particular good and the comprehensive good. The least that can be said is that in most cases this perception takes place in and through the complex process of deliberation. Without a phase of indecision and deliberation, no matter how short we please to imagine it, the discrepancy between the particular good and the comprehensive good is not perceived or is perceived in a confused and merely incipient way: consequently, the act which follows is not free, or possesses merely a low degree of freedom. This is indeed how things happen within the limit of ordinary experience.

The problem is to determine the nature of the necessity by reason of which indeliberate judgments, or most of them, are deprived of indifference. One thing is sure: this necessity is not metaphysical. Yet deliberation, which is a discursive process, and the phase of indetermination in which the deliberative discourse takes place, are made necessary only by the factor of potentiality which affects the intellect and the will of man. This factor of potentiality is an obstacle to freedom rather than a cause of freedom.

Let us raise the question: is deliberation necessary to the indifference of the judgment? The question has two aspects: (*a*) Deliberation is a way to achieve the perception of the discrepancy between the particular good and the comprehensive good. The thing necessary for the indifference of the judgment is this advertence. If advertence, which plainly can be achieved through deliberation, can also be achieved through some other method, then deliberation is not necessary to the indifference of the judgment, and an indeliberate action can be free. (*b*) The need for deliberation, whenever actually experienced, is traceable to potentiality in the human mind and will.

In the first chapter of this treatise we recalled that the idea of freedom is commonly accompanied by images of disorder. Then we tried to show that the principle of freedom resides in the necessary constitution of the will, and that freedom results from a state of superdetermination, not from a lack of determination. We have been removing indefatigably the images which lump together freedom and chance, freedom and nonrationality, freedom and disorder, freedom and ontological deficiency. But why should such images be so obstinate that it should be necessary to remove them again and again? Why is it that so many authors, not all of whom are insignificant, express themselves about freedom in terms of contingency, of indetermination, of doubt, of hesitancy and of wavering, as if it were conceivable that the principle of freedom should reside in the weakness, the deficiency, the inachievement of the will, as if it were conceivable that the free determination should be less than the unique determination? The time has come to consider the background of such general and stubborn illusions, the aspect of truth which causes these errors to look plausible and attractive.

Freedom of choice properly consists in the indifference of practical judgment. Now, there are two kinds of indifference, which are opposed in many respects, and yet are connected by the thin thread of an analogous resemblance which warrants the use of a common term in spite of a danger of confusion. One indifference results from abundance and another from deficiency. There is the indifference of the rich man, who feels sure that he will not lack anything, and that of the poor fellow, for whom all is good, because he has nothing; that of the strong, who feels invulnerable, and that of the weak, who feels incapable of any resistance. There is the indifference of things which are hard, which force their way through any environment without damage, and there is the indifference of things which are soft, which change form at every contact and take on all imprints. One indifference consists in a power to produce a multiplicity of effects, and the other indifference consists in an ability to receive a multiplicity of influences. One kind of indifference is grounded in the accomplishment of being—its perfection, the integrality of its determination, its actuality, and its activity. The other kind of indifference is grounded in the incompleteness of being—its imperfection, its indetermination, its passivity, its potentiality. Briefly: there is such a thing as an active indifference, and there is such a thing as a passive indifference. The amount of passive indifference is inversely proportional to the ontological level of the thing. It reaches its maximum in prime matter—in matter in an absolute sense—which of itself is "neither substance nor quantity nor quality . . . ," which is ready for any form because of itself it is formless. Active indifference reaches its maximum in the will. Freedom is a distinguished case of active indifference.

Cognitive powers are actively indifferent inasmuch as they are able to exercise, within the limits of their distinctive object, acts of an indefinite qualitative diversity. Thus, sight reacts to the unceasing changes of the sensorial environment by sensations which always are, in some degree, things new and unprecedented. But with regard to the very attraction of the act to be accomplished, cognitive powers do not enjoy any indifference; they undergo in necessary fashion the desirability of their own acts. I cannot not see when it is clear and my eyes are open. But the will, at the term of deliberation, is able to will and not to will. Its privilege among the actively indifferent causes consists in the domination that it exercises over the attractive power of its own operations: ultimately the attractiveness of the will's operations, as well as the attractiveness of their object, comes from the will itself. Freedom is not only active indifference: it is dominating indifference.

Yet, not all is determination, actuality, activity, energy, and power in the will of man. Opposite the active and dominating indifference which results from its necessary determination and constitutes its freedom, our will contains a passive indifference which results from its weakness, from its relative indetermination, from the aspect of potentiality that its nature implies. This passive indifference is an obstacle to freedom, but by reason of the analogical connection mentioned in the foregoing, there is here a deceptive resemblance between the power which is supposed to overcome the obstacle and the obstacle that the power is supposed to overcome. By dominating indifference the human will is an image of God; by passive indifference it rather is an image of prime matter. Aquinas mentions a philosopher who "most foolishly" thought that God was the prime matter. Without going so far many people handle analogical intellection so clumsily that they confuse free choice with the passive indifference of the will.

Yet, in order to remove the danger of such a confusion, it suffices to think of what the predominance of passive indifference means in terms of concrete psychology. Passive indifference is to the will what doubt is to the intellect, and just as firm judgment implies the elimination of doubt by knowledge, so every decision implies that passive indifference is defeated by active indifference. If passive indifference resists, the will remains in a state of suspense. The passive indifference of the will is known to all under the familiar names of irresolution, perplexity and indecision. In Hamlet, thought is constantly busy feeding the resistance of irresolution. Morbidly maintained and expanded, passive indifference kills action and kills freedom. The prodigal child of André Gide, who on his return to the house of the father regrets the good time when he shared the food of the pigs, would have few admirers if his speeches did not appeal to a tendency secretly present in the heart of all men. As a result of the analogy which connects, in spite of all contrasts, the two kinds of indifference, the charms of indetermination are often mistaken for those of freedom. As soon as man yields to the lure of decadence, he is tempted to substitute the delectations of a state of availability for the strong but costly joys of the mastery of one's self. In the heroes and the saints the sense for freedom is accompanied by a sense of the unique worth of irrevocable decisions. The literary characters who seek mobility in order to avoid decisions do almost exactly the contrary of what the heroes and the saints do. They would be without prestige and without imitators if the cultivation of passive indifference did not procure a cheap substitute of freedom to intellectuals who no longer have any sense of freedom.

To sum up: the discursive act of deliberation is the form commonly assumed by the perception of the discrepancy between the particular good and the comprehensive good. Yet the necessity of deliberation, precisely considered as a discursive act, does not pertain to the essential causes of freedom. Consequently it is impossible to say that freedom never exists in any degree without deliberation. It can be said, indeed, that there is no human freedom without deliberation if, and only if, it is established that deliberation is the method that advertence necessarily assumes in man. An indeliberate practical judgment is capable of indifference if and insofar as it is possible to perceive without deliberation the relation of the particular good to the absolute good. Under ordinary circumstances such a perception is not possible, or if it is possible it is too incomplete to bring about a fully indifferent judgment and a fully free act.

With this specification, it must be said that the conditions of the indifferent judgment are not realized at the starting point of the voluntary process. The indifferent judgment is preceded by a determinate judgment, and an attraction which is merely undergone precedes the attraction which is freely chosen.

The reading of a scientific book has brought forth in my mind the consideration that it would be good to study a certain theory, and through that theory to know a certain truth. This consideration has given birth to a desire. Then and only then do indifferent judgment and free choice become possible. This particular desire is infinitely far from coinciding with the only desire that I experience unconditionally, viz., that of a good which exhausts the universality of the good: already, the practical judgment, which initially was determinate, is suspended by a contrary practical judgment. Deliberation has begun. The disadvantages of the undertaking appear. A thorough study of this theory will take much time, at the expense of my other studies, of my business and of my pleasures; it will demand much night work at the expense of my health; it will make it necessary for me to do some reading for which I am poorly prepared, and so on. The initial desire will be confirmed and followed by execution only if it stands the test of the period of indifference. True, it is easy to consider a great number of cases in which no phase of indifference takes place, in which the desire does not undergo any test, in which the execution follows immediately the determinate judgment and the determinate desire. This is what happens whenever some factor prevents the construction of a judgment opposed to the initial judgment and renders deliberation impossible. This inhibiting factor may be the lack of time, as it happens when a sudden danger makes it necessary to define our conduct in a split second; it may also be a haunting image or an exclusive passion, as it happens in some mentally diseased people and in many people whose health is excellent.

Thus, the broad genus of the acts devoid of freedom, or at least not capable of unqualified freedom, comprises, besides the operations in which the reason plays no part, the initial acts of the will and all the subsequent developments thereof if any lasting obstacle prevents the judgment from having complete access to the state of indifference. Among the inhibiting forces which oppose the indifference of the judgment, the best known pertain to the pathology of the nervous system.[8] The theorist of free choice may have failed to recognize the signif-

[8] The exploration of subconscious and unconscious motivations, pursued with so much success by psychologists of the twentieth century, has cast a doubt in many minds on the reality of free will, or at least on the frequency of free acts. I am conscious of having freely chosen a certain line of conduct for a certain reason. But a day arrives when analysis reveals that the reason avowed by consciousness did not have any influence on my choice; my true reason was altogether different. Drawn by motives of which we are not conscious, are we then free? It seems that the discussion of this very important and good question could be organized by the following principles:

(*a*) An authentic process does not lose any authenticity just because it may be imitated. To use the famous example of Bergson's, a fool may pretend that he is Napoleon. Napoleon pretended the same thing. Their declarations do not have precisely the same value, but the fact that the authentic process can be imitated can always pose problems of identification, sometimes difficult and sometimes impossible to solve. We know with surety that such a sick person, who believes himself to be Napoleon, is not; we are very much less categorical when it is a question of persons in whom one believes to recognize the son of Louis XVI or Czar Alexander. These risks of uncertainty are inseparable from our destiny as intelligent beings constrained to seek nourishment in a world of contingency.

(*b*) There is no doubt that in the ideally perfect exercise of free will the motivation would be entirely conscious. It can hardly be contested that without perfect coincidence between the motive of which I am conscious and the motive which really is effective, liberty is lessened

icance of sociological factors. There are some ways of being bound by the social whole and in the social

---

somewhat. It does not follow at all that it is abolished. The plurality of motives and the indefinite multiplicity of degrees of consciousness make it necessary to conceive of a vast zone of actions of which all one can say is that they are free to a certain degree and that they would be more so if, all other things being equal, their true motives had been more clearly conscious.

(*c*) Must we say then that in the extreme cases the unconscious motive suppresses freedom? Without doubt. Such would seem to be the case of the man who executes a post-hypnotic suggestion: he finds good reasons for his actions and is totally ignorant that the true reason is the influence to which he is subject without having apparently any consciousness of it. It is possible that here the consciousness of freedom might be totally illusory. Similar phenomena can be observed in dreams.

(*d*) The frequency of fully free acts is a subject that is bound to remain mysterious until the end of time. We have only very imperfect means for knowing our own life of freedom. We know even much less well the life of others. This situation entails difficulties in the life of society, especially in the administration of justice, which man must, without letup, work to surmount. The sciences and the humanities could render great services to justice by improving our means of understanding the concrete life of freedom. On the other hand we should note that in a great number of circumstances, and in many respects, it is not important, it is not even desirable, that I know my life of freedom or that of my brother: it suffices that these things are known to God.

(*e*) Finally, against the deterministic prejudices, which

whole—in other words, some forms of sociability—which give the group such a power over the nonrational faculties that a practical judgment contrary to the collective imperatives becomes physically impossible: a host of images and emotions keeps a watch on the threshold of consciousness in order to prevent the construction of such a judgment. The dream of every tyranny is to systematize this form of sociability and to establish in the soul of everyone a pretorian guard over nonrational forces in order to assure the safety of the regime and its smooth operation by destroying the deep center of all freedom, viz., the indifference of the practical judgment.

FREE WILL AND THE PRINCIPLE OF CAUSALITY

We have recognized the mark of reason in all the aspects of freedom. We have also understood that

---

the popularization of the psychological sciences spreads actively among our contemporaries, it is well to recall that the clarity of our consciousness and the risk of being deprived—whether a little or a lot—of our freedom by unconscious forces are matters which are subject, in considerable measure, to our free decisions. There are bad habits and vices which favor ignorance of what happens within us. And there are virtues which make it happen that souls can clearly see into themselves, and there are sciences which, when well understood, place into the hands of these virtues instruments that are more and more effective.

mastery over particular goods results necessarily from the natural constitution which the will owes to its rational origin. It remains for us to consider free will from the point of view of causality. It is perfectly clear that any position concerning the rationality of free will or its foundation in natural necessity is not solidly established as long as the theory which assimilates the free act to an event without cause retains the least appearance of truth. If it were true that the free act is, in any sense whatever, an exception to the principle of causality, then nothing that has preceded would prevent the whole theory of free will from foundering on the absurdities of irrationalism and lawless contingency.

The principle of causality is a subject concerning which scholars and philosophers speak in that grave manner which a well-established fact inspires, as though the whole world were supposed to know what it is about and to understand the expression "principle of causality" in a perfectly definite sense. This pedantic assurance serves to hide our ignorance and our differences. Those who speak concerning the principle of causality usually do not say what it is they are speaking about. Perhaps they would say it if they knew. Often the principle of causality is formulated in such a way, explicitly or implicitly, as to exclude the possibility of free will. Thereafter to say that a free act would be an exception to the principle of causality makes hardly any sense.

What we mean by the principle of causality is a law concerning the relation of effect to cause. It is an obvious abuse and one that loads the dice to call the principle of causality a proposition not concerning the relation of effect to cause, but concerning the uniformity of causal relations and, more generally, concerning the uniformity and legality of natural processes. (It is hardly necessary to mention the magnificent studies of Meyerson on this subject in *Identité et realité.*) As for propositions concerning the causal relation itself, there are some very popular ones which do not say anything at all, e.g., "every effect has its cause." Others involve an awkward ambiguity, e.g., "everything which happens has a cause"; the meaning of the word "a" is uncertain: does this indefinite article leave indeterminate the question of the unity of the cause? or is it perhaps an adjective suggesting that at the origin of everything that happens there is *a* thing endowed with unity? We need only consider these uncertainties in order to understand that the formulation of the principle of causality is a task that requires considerable work. And it is in the experience of change that we find the point of departure for all speculation concerning causes.

The history of scientific and philosophical thought, as well as the psychology of daily life, shows that the first response of the human mind to the problem of change consists in noticing that in the being which changes not everything changes. A part remains the same. We observe a succession of aspects, but these successive aspects are borne by something which remains one and the same through the phases of its becoming. Only sophists pretend that a man is no longer the same when he goes from one place to another.[9] The panorama of the universe is not as disconcerting as it appears at first. Aspects change, but underneath the successive aspects there are things: they make themselves known with such clarity and our mind conceives them with such impressiveness that we do not hesitate to suppose them or to construct them when it is not possible to observe them. Those things which now support one appearance and now another we can consider precisely as *bearers* of appearances or forms: then we call them subjects or substrates, *subjecta, ὑποκείμενα*. We represent them to ourselves as that which lies underneath the forms of becoming, that in which the forms of becoming exercise their uncertain existence.[10] Sometimes we can

[9] See Aristotle, *Physics*, IV, 11, 219b20.

[10] See Aristotle, *Metaphysics*, VIII, 1, 1042a32, and *Physics*, II, 3, 194b23.

consider the totality composed by the subject and its form; in relation to this whole, this composite, the things of which we speak assume the character of an original matter *out of which* things are made. In order to designate *that out of which* things are made, it is convenient to borrow the name of something which serves to make many things. With wood one makes houses, ships, arms, utensils; that out of which things are made is therefore called *materia*, that is to say here, wood.

The recognition of the need for the efficient cause arises at the moment when mind recognizes the insufficiency of an explanation by the material cause. To the extent that a system refuses to acknowledge this insufficiency it must bypass efficient causes, even though it perhaps retains the name. Materialism is never anything but a tendency, the systematic tendency to extract everything possible (and even more) out of the material cause as a principle of explanation. An absolute system of materialism has never been conceived or existed. Such a system would pretend to explain becoming merely by designating the thing out of which things are made. One can make extraordinary concessions to the taste for explanation by the material cause, but one cannot, except by eliminating becoming and annihilating the world of our experience, say that the house is everything which it is because of bricks, and that bricks are everything which they are because of clay. There is still other clay in the unexplored soil, and there are still bricks piled up in the builder's yard which are not a house. In order that there should be bricks, it is necessary that the clay be dug, made uniform in consistency, shaped, and baked in fire. The passive voice of the verbs says very well what we want to say. It signifies that the modifications distinguishing extracted clay from unextracted clay, homogeneous clay from clay mixed with sand, clay shaped into rectangular solids from clay without regular form, cannot be sufficiently explained by the clay: they are received in it, and do not rise up in it in virtue of its identity with itself. Clay can become brick; it is not brick by itself. If it were brick by itself, it would always and in all ways be brick and would not become brick. In order not to eliminate becoming and to annihilate nature, therefore, it is necessary here to pass from same to other. Same does not suffice. *Everything which is in motion is moved by another.*[11] The accent is on the word *other*. The efficient cause is really distinct from "that which is in motion." We shall call this formula of the principle of causality *the principle of the altereity of the cause*.

[11] See Aristotle, *Metaphysics*, I, 3, 984a21, and Saint Thomas, *Summa Theologica*, I, q. 2, a. 3.

This other is first of all conceived as the agent, as the principle of realization, and as a being in act. Why, in fact, was it found impossible, in the analysis of becoming, to keep to the same? What precisely is the reason why the passage to the other is necessary? The thing which has become A could be A, since it has become it. But to say that it could be A means that it was A in a certain manner, that it was A in potentiality. Its *being* A has as its origin its *power to be* A, and so far everything is accounted for by the same. The necessity for the other appears at the moment at which we consider that between being in potentiality and being in act there is properly an immense difference with respect to the quantity of being, or, what amounts to the same thing, with respect to ontological intensity.

Without doubt, potentiality is not pure possibility, but real possibility, existing in a really existing subject. We recognize this by comparing a new-born infant, who is a mathematician in potentiality, with a new-born monkey, who is not. As far as actual geometrical knowledge goes, monkey and infant are equal; they are equally ignorant. Nevertheless, in the order of reality the infant prevails over the monkey on account of his purely potential mathematical knowledge. There is no question of contesting the reality of potentiality. But the mathematical scholar is a mathematician in a more real sense than the new-born infant.

If we give, as the only origin of being in act, being in potentiality, then we place the origin of that addition of reality which distinguishes being in act from being in potentiality in nothing. That is why the subject of change cannot explain all of the change; that is why, in order to safeguard the possibility of change, there has to be, in addition to a *same* which changes and which, by itself, is an altogether potential thing, an *other*, which has the character of an actual thing. *Every agent acts according as it is in act*:[12] this second formulation of the principle of causality we call *the principle of the actuality of the cause*.

More precisely, this other whose actuality makes the change possible by uniting itself with the potentiality of the same, possesses in act *that which* the subject of the change only possesses in potentiality. If the subject of change becomes actual in respect B, to place its origin in a cause provided with actuality in respect A but not in respect B, that would once again place the origin of the addition of reality which distinguishes being in act from being in potentiality in nothing. Therefore the effect resem-

[12] See Aristotle, *Metaphysics*, IX, 8, 1049b24–25, and Saint Thomas, *Contra Gentes*, I, q. 16, a. 4.

bles the cause. *Every agent produces something which resembles itself:*[13] this third formulation of the principle of causality we call *the principle of essential causality*, for only a cause to which the effects are connected by a resemblance is a cause that is in any sense essential.

The principle of causality requires other expressions,[14] but in applying it to the free act these three formulas of altereity, actuality, and resemblance contain, it will be perceived, everything that we need to know in order to decide if free will has the character of an infraction of the law of causality.

1. The living being which moves itself seems, by its very definition, to eschew the principle of the altereity of the cause. But the answer is easy: what characterizes life is the (non-accidental) coincidence of mover and moved in one and the same thing possessing individual unity; the action of life does not require that mover and moved be really

[13] See Aristotle, *loc. cit.*, and Saint Thomas, *De Veritate*, q. 21, a. 4.

[14] In particular, in order to express the entire bearing of the principle of altereity, it is necessary to formulate it not in relation to becoming (as the expressions of Aristotle to which we have referred do—expressions which belong more to philosophical physics than to metaphysics), but in relation to being and its metaphysical modes: unity and plurality (*Summa Theologica*, I, q. 3, a. 7).

identical in all respects: a being which moves itself is composed of parts and within the individual unity there is a real distinction between mover and moved. (In God, where being does not imply parts, life does not consist in a movement or any action whatever: in the immovable actuality of divine perfection, the essence of life is realized with infinitely greater authenticity than in life in the mode of motion.[15])

Thus, wherever life consists in movement or actualization the principle of altereity of the cause is verified thanks to the duality of the moving part and the moved part. These views apply without particular difficulty to psychic life, as long as the notions of whole and part are not arbitrarily tied to what spatial imagination can give us. It has often been pretended that it is impossible to distinguish a plurality of faculties in the soul without contradicting what is otherwise taught concerning the simplicity and spirituality of the soul. Those who uphold this objection do not, however, hesitate to speak of "the fruitful reflections" of an inquirer, i.e. of an active reasoner, who "takes advantage of what he knows." In fact, to reason is to take advantage of what one knows; more precisely—for it may be a case of a practical matter—it is to utilize,

[15] *Summa Theologica,* I, q. 18, aa. 1, 2, 3.

for the sake of new knowledge, knowledge already actually possessed. It is to help oneself with what one already knows in order to reach knowledge of what one does not yet know. In expressing oneself thus, one affirms that there is in the mind an actual part—mind insofar as it is determined by knowledge already possessed—and a potential part—mind insofar as it is determinable by the knowledge it does not yet possess—and that the first part brings about the actualization of the second. In order that the application of the notion of whole and part to soul and mind cease being disconcerting, it is enough to consider that the quantitative whole, whose parts are external to one another and which are distinguished from one another, in the absence of any qualitative variety, by their very position, is only one of the terms of the analogical series designated by the word "whole." Another term of the same series, less familiar but no less real and no less intelligible, is the dynamic whole whose parts are the diverse faculties of a subject or more generally its diverse real possibilities. In the reasoner, the mover and the moved are dynamic parts, really distinct, of the intellect: one part is an actualized possibility (through knowledge of the premises); the other part is an actualizable possibility (through knowledge of the conclusion).

In the same manner, by a distinction of dynamic parts, the principle of altereity of the cause is verified in the free act. Here, as in the reasoning intellect, the mover and the moved are really distinct possibilities of the same faculty. In the same way in which, in reasoning, the intellect, by virtue of its determination through knowledge of principles, moves the intellect that is still potential with respect to the conclusion, just so the will, in its movement of adhering to a particular good which is the object of free choice, is moved by the will acting in virtue of its fundamental determination by the universal essence of good. When spiritual faculties put themselves in act, the mover and the moved are really distinct, but their distinction is contained within the limits of the individual unity: for we are dealing with a vital act. Furthermore, mover and moved are only distinguished as dynamic parts of the same principle of immanent activity: we have to do therefore with special cases where life takes on a particular intimacy.

2. For a reason which will become clear in a moment we believe that we should modify the order of the formulas of the principle of causality and consider the principle of resemblance before the principle of actuality.

To say that there exists a resemblance between

the (essential) cause and the effect, is to say that the cause acts *according to* a formal determination in which the intelligible outline of the effect can be recognized, or again, what amounts to the same thing, according to a formal predetermination of the action and the effect. It is not at all necessary that there be resemblance between the cause as thing and the effect as thing: such resemblance does not exist except in the case in which the causation concerns the substantial being of what is caused—that is to say, in the case of generation (a man engenders a man). In all other cases, the caused and the cause are or can be things of different kinds (a man makes a chair), but the action of the cause is none the less rendered such and such (qualified, specified) by a directing form or *idea,* which is found again in the effect. The chair does not resemble the cabinet-maker considered in his substantial being, but it does resemble the directing plan which is present in the mind of the artisan and *according to* which he exercises his power. This is a very important aspect of the theory of causality which, paradoxically, appears to have escaped Meyerson.

When by an act of the will I produce an exterior change, or when the believer attributes a phenomenon to divine intervention (we have shown above that these are connected concepts), it is certain that one does not hesitate at all to speak of cause and effect. Yet, there is here no possible identity, and, what is more, I have immediate intuition of this. Not for a single moment can I nourish the illusion that my will is something analogical to the movement which it produces; there is here a concept of causality fundamentally different from that which we have studied and which is founded on identity. In order to mark this distinction, we shall designate this latter concept as that of *scientific causality,* and shall apply to the former the term *theological causality,* since after all, as we have seen, it is the supposition of divinity in the events of nature that sets it to work.[16]

When by an act of the will I produce an exterior change such as putting my pen in contact with the blank page, there is no possible identity between the will as a spiritual thing and the movement of the pen as a physical thing. But it is to the form by which the will causes the movement that the movement ought to be related.[17] This form is the practical judgment, extended in imagination to include the plan for motion. Between the practical judgment "it is necessary to trace on the blank paper the signs which conventionally represent the ideas of *identity* and *reality*" and the movement by which

[16] Emile Meyerson, *Identité et realité,* third edition (Paris: Alcan, 1926), p. 42.

[17] *Summa Theologica,* I, q. 41, a. 5.

the words *identity, reality* are traced, the resemblance, if not identity, is manifest.

In place of an exterior movement commanded by a free choice, let us direct now our inquiry to free choice itself as an interior event and as an immanent act of the will. Between the cause of this act and this act itself, is there a relation of resemblance? Here again, consideration of the practical judgment furnishes the answer. Let us observe the act of free choice at the moment when it has been fully made: only then does it possess fully the character of an effect. It is a composite of which the practical judgment is the formal part. It is then a question of knowing, if, in the production of the free choice, the will has acted *according to* the same form—that is to say, according to the same practical judgment. For example, at the end of a deliberation, I have decided to go to Paris rather than to Montpellier in order to study medicine. As long as the deliberation lasts, the judgments "I should go to Paris" and "I should go to Montpellier" are both present; then the judgment "I should go to Paris" receives the dignity of the last practical judgment, and this dignity is given to it by the will. Thus we want to know according to what form the will acts when it determines itself by making the judgment "I should go to Paris"—

the last practical judgment and the end of the deliberation.

According to all the evidence, it is not in acting according to the judgment "I should go to Montpellier" that the will has conferred to the judgment "I should go to Paris" the dignity of the last practical judgment. It is in acting according to the judgment "I should go to Paris" that it has determined itself alone according to that judgment. From a slightly different point of view, let us record the division of the will into a dynamic moved part and a dynamic moving part: the dynamic moved part receives, as its form, the practical judgment "I should go to Paris," and it is in acting according to this same judgment that the dynamic moving part causes the informing of the dynamic moved part. There is therefore a perfect resemblance between the form of the cause and the form of the effect. In truth, the causal process takes place here in such extreme conditions of intimacy that between the form of the cause and the form of the effect there is more than resemblance: between the practical judgment according to which the moving will acts, and the practical judgment by which the moved will is informed, there is complete identity, numerical unity. It is the same judgment, purely and simply. The principle of resemblance here applies according to a mode that is superior to that of simple resemblance.

3. As far as our inquiry has progressed, we have been aware that the difficulties concerning the principle of altereity and the principle of resemblance were mixed up, in the final analysis, with those which concern the principle of actuality. These then are the final difficulties, and it is proper to consider them last.

These difficulties are generally exposed in the Leibnizian, and essentially ambiguous, language of sufficient reason. It is very easy to formulate the principle of sufficient—or as Leibniz always called it, determining—reason, in such a manner as to make sure from the beginning the affirmation of universal determinism and the exclusion of free will. It is of little interest to ask, under those conditions, if free will is compatible with the principle of sufficient reason. It would be much more important to submit the notion of sufficient reason to a critical examination. By holding fast to the principle of causality as it has been formulated above we are certain to avoid all begging of principle (*petitio principii*). Furthermore, if there exists a principle of rationality (for we must avoid in all respect the odious equivocation expressed by the words "sufficient reason") that is irreducible to the principles of identity, of material causality, of efficient causality and final causality, such a principle has a distinct role only with respect to purely logical emanations: it does not apply to the case of free will except by taking the form of the principle of the actuality of the cause. It is thus in relation to this principle that we shall consider the difficulties ordinarily related to the principle of sufficient reason.

The will is pictured as drawn by motives of unequal force. Is it free to choose between them? Let us suppose that it chooses the weaker one. There is more actuality in the stronger motive, in the greater good, than in the weaker motive and the lesser good. If the weaker motive prevails, the will acts according to the line of less actuality. There is, no doubt, goodness and actuality on both sides, but if the side of less actuality and more potentiality prevails, is it not necessary to say that the agent acts *according as he is in potentiality*? Let us take as an example a man who, in order to assuage his hatred, commits a crime. He does not believe that he has any chance of escaping punishment. Thus, having to choose between a moment of satisfaction at the price of perpetual imprisonment and a normal or happy life at the price of an effort (painful, no doubt, but, after all, very limited), he chooses the moment of hateful satisfaction. Considering the things in themselves, the good chosen is the lesser good. But was it not the greater good for this man, if account is taken of his character and all the good reasons which he has for hating and for revenging himself? Freedom thus would be reduced to the power of being ourselves in our desires. Our individual being would have the property of coloring the situation in such a fashion that a good could be greater for us, by reason of the accidents of our history, in spite of the nature of the things and natural finalities. Thus conceived, freedom would only escape from the necessity of essential determinations in order to be identified with the necessity of accomplished facts and collections of facts. It would be brought back to an individual and gloriously anarchic spontaneity, but it would be totally deprived of that mastery in which we have recognized the essence of free will. The theory of determination by the strongest motive, even if it makes a great deal of room for individual history in the constitution of this motive and is accompanied with all sorts of subtleties designed to enhance the distinction of unique actions, will never be anything except a variety of determinism.

And yet, to say that a motive *prevails* is to say that in a certain sense—to be defined with extreme care—this motive is the strongest. To say that a good is in fact chosen is to say that it gets the better of rival goods; to say that it gets the better of them is to say that, in some sense, it is greater and more powerful. The question is how to know if the good chosen possesses the greater power anteriorly to the choice and independently of the act of choosing, or if it acquires it through the effect of the choice and does not possess it until the moment when it is chosen. It is only a question, when all is said and done, of knowing if the will can confer on a good (can give it, as one gives a gift to a friend, i.e. gratuitously), by the exercise of its mastery, that character of being greatest. And all the difficulty consists in the appearance of a conflict between such a gratuitous gift and the principle of the actuality of a cause.

I suppose that in the course of a conversation I feel the desire to tell a story that is not very charitable. Matters contrary to charity can be very amusing and in that way constitute a good; but an aspect of non-goodness clearly accompanies this particular good. To comply with charity by remaining silent is a good action which also presents an aspect of non-goodness since it is contrary to certain of my desires. If I speak, I shall give myself a moment of lively pleasure at the price of a very great injury, perhaps infinitely great. If I am silent, I shall live according to charity: there is nothing better. The particular goods to which these two judgments are related ("It is good to tell this story" and "It is good not to tell this story") are immensely unequal and I am fully conscious of this. I know that I would be ridiculous to prefer a moment of malicious pleasure to the good of charity. And nevertheless it happens to us that we tell uncharitable stories in full recognition of the case. I shall tell the story and choose the lesser of two particular goods,[18] if I put my happiness in an instant of malicious pleasure.

Sometimes a spontaneous expression of ordinary language makes a philosophic thought stand out with admirable neatness. We must believe that common sense has a profound understanding of freedom, when it uses the expression "put my happiness in . . .": no philosopher could have found one more adequate. To put one's happiness in a particular good is to give to a particular good the additional quantity of goodness it needs in order

[18] It is in the order of nature that there are here two goods and that the object chosen has the character of a lesser good. Morally, of the two acts between which I have to choose, one is good, and the other is bad. The moral evil is not simply a lesser good. But there is necessarily something good in the object of the morally bad act.

to make itself desirable, absolutely speaking, to the rational appetite. But whence do I draw the power of adding to the goodness of things, to their desirability? In technical language, I draw this power from my adherence to the universal essence of good. In more familiar language, the question would be "how does it happen that I can put my happiness where I want?" and the answer is "I can put my happiness where I will *because I will to be happy*." If it is true, in other words, that the will desires happiness necessarily, and if it is true that all concrete goods that are presented to it are particular goods mixed with non-goodness, then it follows that the voluntary agent has the power of putting his happiness where he pleases—or, what comes to the same thing, of adding to the desirability of a particular good to the point of making it into an absolutely desirable good.

In producing this surplus of goodness the will brings it about that the judgment relative to such a particular good is the last judgment. Every difficulty is gathered together in this crucial act by which the will brings it about that a certain practical judgment terminates the deliberation and constitutes the decision. This operation cannot be without foundation, without reason; it is impossible that it be a product of indetermination, an absurdity, a causal emanation not according to act but according to potency. It is necessary then to designate the force or energy which makes this operation possible.

We want to know how the principle of the actuality of the cause is verified in the act by which the will brings it about that the last practical judgment is the last. What then is the actuality according to which it acts here? Where do we find that reserve of actuality, of energy, which the will can use in order to accomplish this act that is imperceptible and, in a most proper sense of the word, decisive to bring it about that a certain judgment be last? If it comes from the side of the particular object, it seems, at first sight, that determination by the greatest good or by the most powerful motive follows inevitably. But there is here an illusion due to an improper statement of the problem. The determinism of the greatest good does not follow. Nothing follows. Nothing happens. Deliberation is prolonged indefinitely. Neither the greatest nor the least good, since both are mixed with non-good, attracts the will determinately. The true question is "under what condition does a particular good become unconditionally desirable for a rational appetite?" This condition is the same for the greatest good and for the least good. It is no less necessary in the case of the greatest good than in the case of the least good, and its realization does not present any more difficulties in the case of the least good than in the case of the greatest good. In both cases equally, it is in the will that we find the energy which the object lacks. In stopping the deliberation, in bringing it about that such a judgment is last, the will acts according to the actuality which its adherence to the universal essence of the good confers on it. The use of this actuality is no less necessary in the case of the greatest good than in the case of a good incomparably smaller. It is in virtue of this actuality that the will is free to act or not to act with regard to a very small good or with regard to a very great good. Because of its natural determination it possesses enough actuality to add to the least of particular goods all the surplus of goodness which it needs in order to be found constituted of absolutely desirable good. Its natural determination makes the will capable of practicing, with regard to all particular goods, its policy of the gratuitous gift, wherein is verified the principle of the actuality of the cause according to the mode that is proper to the free cause.[19]

[19] Jacques Maritain, *A Preface to Metaphysics: Seven Lectures in Being* (New York: Sheed and Ward, 1948), fifth lecture, p. 103: "To this potentiality in all creatures

Obstinately, the initial question recurs. We know that the will possesses all the actuality necessary in order to make this or that determinately desirable. One wants to assign a reason to this preference, one demands *why* the choice is made one way rather than another, and one does not perceive that this restless question contains a *petitio principii.* What does this *why* signify? (*a*) One could mean that it relates to a cause sufficiently characterized by altereity, actuality, and resemblance to the effect: the free cause is not excluded, if it presents all these characteristics. If the question is thus understood, it receives the answer: "the will insofar as it adheres to the universal essence of the good and to the prac-

---

and therefore in all created goods corresponds the dominating influence of the will. The will is specified by good as such, that is to say it is unable as soon as it comes into operation to will anything without first tending to a good chosen as absolute. It thus of its own fiat renders efficacious the particular good which the understanding presents to it, and which determines it. For it pours out upon that particular good, of itself wholly incapable of determining it, the superabundant determination it receives from its necessary object, good as such. It gratuitously makes that good purely and simply good for itself—the subject—in virtue, to put it so, of the fullness of intelligible determination with which it overflows. Thus the principle of sufficient reason plays no more magnificent part than its part in making possible the freedom of the will."

tical judgment of its choice is a cause presenting these characteristics and it is free." (*b*) One can mean that the question *why* relates inflexibly to a cause provided with univocal determination. Any discussion framed within such a *petitio principii* is superfluous.

It is useful, however, to understand how the begging of principle is here produced. Efficient causality is divided into free causality and determined causality. The first part of this division constitutes, without doubt, the most intelligible case in itself. But determined causality is less mysterious and, despite certain appearances, more familiarly known than free causality. The begging of the question of which we speak recalls that it is difficult to surmount the influence of a familiar model. It serves to recall that the understanding of freedom demands a new effort and a fresh mind. A little while ago, tired minds only understood "classical determinism"; nowadays, many among them show preferences for an indeterministic vision that is borrowed from physics according to the procedures of doubtful logic.

Few thinkers ever awoke to the theory that freedom is superdetermination rather than indetermination, and that its principle is more highly and more certainly *formed* than that of determinate causality; freedom proceeds, not from any weakness, any imperfection, any feature of potentiality on the part of the agent but, on the contrary, from a particular excellence in power, from a plenitude of being and an abundance of determination, from an ability to achieve mastery over diverse possibilities, from a strength of constitution which makes it possible to attain one's end in a variety of ways. In short, freedom is an active and dominating indifference. Whereas the line of spontaneity or "from-withinness" leads to the notion of the voluntary, it is the line of *actuality in causal power* which leads to the notion of free choice.

Whether or not it is possible at all to express the principle of causality in a single formula, a plurality of expressions effectively helps to secure an exact understanding of this principle. For one thing, the notion of cause is primarily relative to the world of change which constitutes the first object of our intellect; accordingly, the primary expression of the principle of causality is relative to becoming, and describes the cause as necessary to the existence of any change, of any event, of any thing that comes into existence. By reason of this essential reference to change, such an expression of cause and of the principle of causality remains physical, and belongs to the philosophy of nature rather than to metaphysics. It is only in an ulterior phase of elaboration that cause and the principle of causality are expressed in terms of being *qua* being and refer to accomplished existence as well as to the process of coming into existence. Without the duality of the physical and the metaphysical formulas, cause and the principle of causality would never be the subject of a metaphysical consideration—or if they were, their metaphysical treatment would ignore the law of order in analogical sets which alone can insure the experimental foundation of metaphysics, and makes the difference between metaphysical science and the questionable products of metaphysical imagination. Moreover, whether causality is considered physically or metaphysically, the diverse aspects of cause and of its relation to effect are best expressed by a diversity of formulas. After having asserted that every union of things really diverse, as well as every event, demands a cause, the notion of cause and the relation of cause to effect are specified in terms of actuality, in terms of resemblance, and in terms of otherness. "Every agent acts according as it is in act" traditionally expresses the principle of the actuality of the cause; "every agent produces a thing similar to itself" expresses the principle of resemblance between cause and effect, which can also be termed principle of essential causality, for it holds in the case of the essential cause and by no means in a relation of accidental causality; "whatever is in motion is moved by something else" expresses the principle of the otherness of the cause. Of these three, the principle of actuality is the first and the most fundamental. True, the human mind, in its primary endeavor to explain change, is led to efficient causality by the insufficiency of the material cause, by the insufficiency of the thing potential, by the impossibility of deriving change, without further ado, from the ability of a bearer to stand a succession of forms, or from the permanence of that which proves able to be formed in diverse ways and to enter a diversity of composites. When a lump of clay becomes a work of art, the process can be traced, indeed, to the potency of the clay, but not without further ado. What the principle of efficient causality primarily says is that change requires, no less certainly than the potency of whatever is in change, a being in act, a thing which, just as matter causes change by way of potency, should cause change by way of act and account for the difference between the actuality of change and the mere ability to change—a difference in which the metaphysician recognizes a particular case of the contrast between "to be" and "not to be."

Every agent acts according as it is in act; no agent ever acts according as it is in potency, but the actuality of the cause admits of degrees. The actuality by reason of which an agent acts may be more or less of an actuality, it may be more or less complete, more or less intense, it may cover more or less ground, it may include a smaller or a larger multitude of virtualities; in short, it may be characterized either by relative poverty or by plenitude. The center of the problem of freedom lies precisely here. The decisive issue is whether freedom results from particularly weak or from particularly strong actuality on the part of the cause. In a remarkable variety of contexts—philosophic, theological, moral, scientific, psychological, and literary—it has been held that the poorer the actuality of the cause, the better its chance to act freely. A person ready to do wrong as well as to do right would enjoy a distinguished degree of freedom, far superior to whatever freedom, if any, is enjoyed by the souls that have been simple enough to let themselves be confined within the limits of virtue. Indeed, many people fear that if they become stabilized in the good their freedom will be curtailed, and such curtailment they hate so much that to assert and maintain what they consider their freedom they choose to commit, once upon a while, wrong actions in which they are not particularly interested. The "gratuitous act" so popular in modern literature—e.g., to throw out of the window of a train a gentleman whom you have never seen before—is a striking literary expression of a theory also represented in domains where fancy is supposed not to be tolerated. From the consideration that a causal or deterministic process is predictable, it is commonly inferred that unpredictability is the measure of freedom. Such a view has been applied to the whole hierarchy of nature: there would be more freedom in a dog than in a chemical because, within our ability to define the circumstances, the behavior of a chemical can be predicted with incomparably more certitude than that of a dog. When this approach is applied to human affairs, it entails the puzzling consideration that the most free of men are also the most unpredictable, from which anyone can infer that, for the smooth operation of our business, there should not be too many free men among our associates. In close relation to these views, let us recall the theory, so common among social scientists, that if social science were complete and ignorance totally routed, liberty would disappear together with our hesitancies, our trials and errors, and our arbitrariness. More than one social scientist, having remained intuitively, emotionally, and morally dedicated to liberty, wishes, at the bottom of his heart, that social science should always be so imperfect as to leave plenty of room for trials and errors and for the arbitrariness of individual preference.

In the language of moral psychology, indetermination is termed irresolution or perplexity. To apprehend the true relation of freedom to causality, it is helpful to ask this simple question: "where do we find the most unmistakable examples of whatever we call freedom, free choice, free will, liberty?" Do we find these distinguished examples in perplexed, irresolute, weak-willed and highly suggestible people? Or should we consider as the most certain exemplifications of the free man persons in firm control of their images and emotions, persons who know what they want and who will not be deterred from their goals by accidents of imagination or affectivity, pressure or lure, disease or poverty; persons who, at the summit of human energy, hold that death itself is an accident which cannot affect their relation to the really important ends of human life?

BOOKS BY YVES R. SIMON

1. *Introduction à l'ontologie du connaître*. Paris, 1934. Reprinted 1965 by Brown Reprint Library, Dubuque, Iowa.
2. *Critique de la connaissance morale*. Paris, 1934.
3. *La Campagne d'Ethiopie et la pensée politique Française*. Paris, 1936.
4. *Trois leçons sur le travail*. Paris, 1938.
5. *Nature and Functions of Authority*. Milwaukee, 1940.
6. *La grande crise de la République Française*. Montreal, 1941.
7. *La Marche à la délivrance*. New York, 1942. English edition: *The March to Liberation*. Milwaukee, 1942.
8. *Prévoir et savoir*. Montreal, 1944.
9. *Par delà l'expérience du désespoir*. Montreal, 1945. English edition: *Community of the Free*. New York, 1947.
10. *Philosophy of Democratic Government*. Chicago, 1951. Phoenix Books paperback edition: Chicago, 1961.
11. *Traité du libre arbitre*. Liège, 1951. The present volume incorporates a revised translation into English of this work.
12. *A General Theory of Authority*. Notre Dame, 1962.
13. *The Tradition of Natural Law*, edited by Vukan Kuic. New York, 1965. Spanish edition: *La Tradición de la Ley Natural*. Madrid, 1968.
14. *Freedom and Community*, edited by Charles P. O'Donnell. New York, 1968.

Index